MW01100276

The Rise and Fall of ISIS
And Those Who Will Lead the Islamic Caliphate

Best Wishes,

Mark S. Hoffmeister

THE RISE AND FALL OF ISIS
AND THOSE WHO WILL LEAD THE ISLAMIC CALIPHATE

MARK S. HOFFMEISTER

The Rise and Fall of ISIS
And Those Who Will Lead the Islamic Caliphate

ISBN: 9781533174680

©2016 Mark Hoffmeister

Unless otherwise noted, all Scripture passages are from the King James Version of the Bible.

Holy Bible, New International Version®, NIV® Copyright ©1973, 1978, 1984, 2011 by Biblica, Inc.® Used by permission. All rights reserved worldwide.

DEDICATION

This book is dedicated to
all those who have accepted Jesus Christ as their Savior
and look to Him in times of trouble.

ACKNOWLEDGEMENTS

I am grateful to Rob Fischer for editing this book for me. He has been a tremendous help and his diligent work has helped me tremendously.

I also appreciate Heather Wilbur whose creative genius graces the cover.

I would like to thank my wife Kelly for her constant support during the time it took to write this book. Kelly has been a constant source of blessing and inspiration to me.

As always, I am thankful for the support of my children who have constantly encouraged me to continue writing.

Many thanks to each of you.

TABLE OF CONTENTS

About the time of the end,
a body of men will be raised up
who will turn their attention to the prophecies,
and insist upon their literal interpretation,
in the midst of much clamor and opposition.

Sir Issac Newton

CHAPTER ONE
THE FINGERPRINT OF EVIL

On Friday the thirteenth, November 2015, a series of horrendous attacks rocked the city of Paris, France. Meticulously timed and executed with fanatical precision, the attacks stunned the nation of France and the international community with their brutality and wanton disregard for life. When the smoke cleared, 127 people were dead and hundreds more were wounded.

Was this just an isolated incident, or one more attack in an orchestrated series of crimes against humanity? The group that claimed responsibility for the violence was ISIS (Islamic State of Iraq and Syria). This is a group that seems to be the epitome of evil, one that rose from the nefarious shell of al-Qaeda with a determination to wreak havoc on all around them. There is no one they will not kill to enforce their fanatical brand of tyranny. Since the creation of ISIS in April 2013, there is no evil they will not perpetrate to ensure total compliance to their wishes. How do you deal with a group like ISIS?

Some in the political arena have said the ISIS is being contained and its influence is not expanding. Is that really the case? Are we being honest with ourselves if we say what we hope is true and then treat our pronouncements as though they were reality? Shouldn't we look at the cold, hard facts to determine what is really happening?

With minimal research it becomes obvious to even the most hardened skeptic that ISIS is far from controlled and is even expanding its sphere of influence in the Levant and surrounding areas. How did this happen? What unique set of circumstances led to the formation of a murderous cult like ISIS, and why have their actions been tolerated and sometimes encouraged by many in the Islamic world? What does the future hold in store for ISIS?

What does the Bible have to say about the resurgence of an Islamic empire that wants to rule the world? Were these events unforeseen, or were they clearly detailed and enumerated by the Word of God? If these events were elaborated upon in the Bible, then how are we failing to recognize the clear scenario taking place before us? Have we been conditioned to look for something else to the point that we fail to recognize what is happening right before our eyes? Are our expectations blinding us so we do not see what is taking place all around us?

There are answers to these questions. One problem is that many of the answers we seek require a paradigm shift and an open mind so we can see things we may have never considered before. In many cases, what we expect to happen will cause us to dismiss anything that does not fit in our worldview. This blind spot can cause us to miss very crucial events and creates a "normalcy bias" that can be detrimental to us.

Here's an example of what I mean by "normalcy bias." On August 29th, 2005, Hurricane Katrina slammed into the Gulf Coast and New Orleans causing untold devastation and loss of life. Why was this storm so deadly? The residents that stayed behind to weather the storm had been clearly warned of the danger. When asked why they stayed behind, many of the residents of New Orleans stated they had been through many storms before, and thought that they were prepared for the strong winds and storm surge of Katrina. Their concept of a "normal" storm, their "normalcy bias," did not prepare them for the onslaught of Hurricane Katrina.

The tides and hurricane force winds caused the storm surge to overwhelm New Orleans' levee system. The fierce storm inundated the city with water and toppled buildings and trees. Only then did it become obvious to anyone left in the city that they were totally unprepared for this monstrous beast of a storm. It was far worse than anyone imagined. Their normalcy bias prevented many from taking the appropriate actions and had devastating consequences for those left in New Orleans.

Do we have a "normalcy bias" toward the Bible—a bias that prevents us from seeing what God's Word tells us about the events happening in His land? Has what we have read in popular books conditioned us? Do we only look for scenarios consistent with the viewpoint espoused in those books and dismiss other viewpoints because they are inconsistent with what we have read?

Most of us have a westernized view of God's Word. We have not grown up in the Holy Land, and are unfamiliar with the customs, cities and culture of the Middle East. In essence, we have an Americanized view of the Scriptures. There is nothing wrong with that—it just means that we have some gaps in our knowledge and some things we need to learn in order to fully understand what the Bible says. The Bible was written in the culture of the Middle East. Understanding cultural idiosyncrasies common to the Middle East can enhance our understanding and provide key insights that we may have never considered before.

What if I were to tell you that the Bible is not silent on the rise of a fanatical power base in Islamic circles? Could it be that God's Word has diligently detailed the fate of all those who want to control this power, including ISIS? What if through our study of the Bible we could determine the fate of a group such as ISIS? What if we could do this not because we are blessed with a gift of prophesy or intuition, but because of what the Bible says is going to happen in this area? As events seem to spin out of control and chaos and uncertainty rampage all around us, such insight would be a tremendous source of comfort and peace of mind.

The Bible does indeed provide us with many insights and details on what is going on in the Middle East right now. But the key to recognizing these facts requires that we assume a "Middle Eastern" perspective, and then carefully study and analyze all the information we have at hand. With this premise in mind, let's take a careful look at the rise of ISIS, and see if we can discover the power base behind their ascension to prominence.

CHAPTER TWO
THE RISE OF ISIS

ISIS seemed to rise from nowhere, and catapulted itself upon the scene with violence unprecedented since the Nazis in WWII. The man orchestrating this current violence was viewed as an unremarkable man by his colleagues, an unassuming and timid man. He was certainly not someone we would expect to lead the most brutal and sadistic power structure on earth today. He was born as Ibrahim Awad Ibrahim al-Badri on the 28th of July, 1971 near the town of Samarra, Iraq. People who knew him as a young child described him as shy and unimpressive, and as someone who was not prone to violence. He became known as a religious scholar, and lived in a mosque in Tobchi, which is on the outskirts of Baghdad.

In his younger years, this man who would emerge as the leader of ISIS was virtually unknown. One of the few people that knew him at the Islamic University said, "We studied the same course, but he wasn't a friend. He was quiet and retiring. He spent time alone...he was insignificant.

He used to lead prayer in a mosque near my area. No one really noticed him."[1]

What happened to the quiet young man that changed him into a monster capable of some of the worst excesses in violence ever witnessed on the earth? What caused him to change his views on violence and to wholeheartedly embrace the slaughter of his fellow human beings with a zeal unseen since Adolf Hitler?

While we cannot say for sure, we may gain some insight by looking at what he was studying right before he had such a profound change of heart. As a young man, Ibrahim Awad Ibrahim al-Badri began an in depth reading of Islamic end-time events. He enrolled in an Islamic University for his undergraduate work and then continued his studies at the University of Baghdad where he earned his doctorate degree in Islamic studies. These were the critical days when Islamic end-time doctrines coalesced in Ibrahim's heart and changed his actions forever. He was obsessed with Muslim teachings that told of a powerful leader who would rise to lead the Islamic world. This leader would direct Islamic forces in a decisive victory over the forces of Rome in the Muslim version of Armageddon known as "Dabiq." The key to this leader's success would be his ability to unite Islamic armies into a coherent fighting force.

Through his studies he realized that the only way to unite the main body of Muslim believers was to resurrect an institution that had been dismantled ninety years earlier at the hands of Mustafa Kemal Ataturk in Turkey. This was the key to controlling the power structure that he so desperately craved. This would be crucial in bringing about "Dabiq."

---

1   Ruth Sherlock, "How a Talented Footballer Became the World's Most Wanted Man, Abu Bakr al-Baghdadi," *The Telegraph*, 11 November 2014. Retrieved 27 December 2014.

What was the institution that empowered the Muslim religion with a united voice and leadership, speaking for all of Islam? It was the office of the Caliphate. Only the office of the Caliphate had the authority to direct the actions of believers in Islam. When the Caliphate spoke and issued a decree, it was incumbent on every Muslim believer to follow and carry out those orders without questioning. If they failed to do so, Islamic believers were subject to death and eternal damnation by Allah. The Caliphate exercised absolute control over the body of Muslim believers. Controlling the Caliphate was the key to controlling the events in the Middle East.

What exactly is the "Caliphate" and how did it come about? How did the Caliphate rise to such an imposing position in the life of an Islamic believer? To answer these questions we have to look at history during the time of the founder of Islam's death. That person was Muhammad. Muhammad brought forth the Islamic religion and ruled the Muslim world with an iron fist. He was the author of the Quran, and the undisputed leader of Islam. When Muhammad died in 632 AD, a huge problem arose. Who was to succeed Muhammad? Who was to lead the Islamic faith with the same authority and power that Muhammad possessed?

Most in the Muslim world suggested that the strongest leader should take over leadership of Islam. The proponents of this succession philosophy named the new leader the "caliph" (successor), and the office that was empowered with the same authority as Muhammad was called the "Caliphate."

The Caliphate was the Muslim world's way of carrying on the leadership of Muhammad. What the man who would become the leader of ISIS discovered was that the office of the Caliphate united the Muslim world in a way that nothing else could. Without the Caliphate, the Muslim world was a hodgepodge of separate nations struggling to survive and constantly at war with each other. When the Islamic world came together under the leadership of the Caliphate, the results were remarkable. National differences seemed to melt away into insignificance, and the Muslim world achieved things they never could have dreamed before, including the subjugation of vast portions of the civilized world under Islamic control.

The Abbasid Dynasty was the perfect example of things that could be accomplished by the direction of a strong caliph running the Caliphate. The Abbasid Dynasty derived its name from Abbas, who was an uncle of the prophet Muhammad. The Abbasid caliphs were all descendants of Abbas who ruled the Islamic world from 750 to 935. Their capital city was Baghdad. And from the streets of Baghdad the Abbasid Dynasty turned the office of the Caliphate into something to be admired by the rest of the Muslim world. The Islamic religion increased and their control over the rest of the world expanded to an unprecedented degree.

The Abbasid Dynasty Caliphates controlled areas from Afghanistan into India, almost the entire Middle East, Northern Africa with expansion into Spain and a foothold in Europe that threatened all the European powers. This Caliphate was so successful that they even sacked the city of Rome and the Vatican in 856, although they were not able to maintain control of this part of Europe.[2]

This was the golden age of Islam. The Abbasid Caliphates ushered in an age of advancement that was unparalleled in the Muslim world. Islamic scholars were the envy of the world because of their advancements in science and

---

2   SF Fleming, *Islam and New Global Realities* (Surprise, AZ: Selah Publishing Group, 2002) p. 81-82.

mathematics. Literature flourished, and different literary styles like 1001 Arabian Nights flourished. Advancements were made in medicine also as the Arab physician Rhases described and attempted to treat smallpox, the plague and a host of other different infectious diseases.

The office of the Caliphate continued on after the demise of the Abbasid Dynasty until it eventually ended up in Turkey with the conquest of Constantinople by the first Turkish caliph Mehmed II in 1453.[3] After him, the office of the Caliphate remained in Turkey (Ottoman Empire) until it was abolished on March 3rd, 1924 by Mustafa Kemal. He later assumed the name Ataturk, and became the leader of Turkey. The last official caliph, Abdulmecid II, was deposed by Turkey's leader Mustafa Kemal Ataturk in 1924.

The man who would become the leader of ISIS saw all of these things captured on the pages of history. Through his studies he realized the only way to unite the Islamic world into a powerful fighting force was to reinstate the office of the Caliphate. But how was he going to do that? The Caliphate had been officially dissolved over ninety years ago. He needed a plan to put himself in a position of power where he could eventually reinstitute the office that controlled the destiny of Islam.

The future leader of ISIS devised a plot to accomplish the thing he desired so much, the office of the Caliphate. There were four mandatory things he needed to accomplish to put himself on target and accomplish his goal:

1. First he needed to get involved in the Islamic struggle (war) against America and the other western powers in Iraq. Only in this way would he be viewed as an important leader.

---

3   Selcuk Akson Somel, *The A to Z of the Ottoman Empire*, (Lanham, MD: Scarecrow Press, 2003), p. 179.

2. Next he needed to be placed in a position of power in the administration of sharia law. Sharia law (religious law set forth in the Quran) governs all Islamic believers. So the one dictating the administration of Sharia law would have power over all other Muslims.

3. At some point in time, he would have to take over the leadership of the group involved in the war against the USA in Iraq (Al-Qaeda). He would have to demonstrate his expertise and leadership by taking over and having complete control. This part was vital in accomplishing his next step.

4. At the proper time, he would have to expand the vision that others had of him and set himself apart. He would have to reinstate the office of the Caliphate, and declare himself the new caliph. In this way he would bring back the power that controlled all of Islam.

THE PATH TO THE CALIPHATE BEGINS

Ibrahim Awad Ibrahim al-Badri, the man who would become the leader of ISIS, set his plan into motion. After the United States invaded Iraq in 2003, he joined al-Qaeda and immediately began fighting against the Americans. He served under Abu Musab al-Zarqawi, and distinguished himself with his abilities to smuggle foreign fighters into Iraq. Because of his proficiency at waging war, al-Zarqawi promoted him as the "emir" (ruler or commander) of Rawa, a town near the Syrian border.

Because of his actions against the United States, Ibrahim al-Badri was arrested by US forces on February 2nd, 2004 and detained at Camp Bucca detention center. Any reservations he had about carrying out his plan disappeared during the time of his internment at Camp Bucca. He became fanatical during his detention and emerged from this time more resolved than ever to strike a blow against any who would oppose him or try to thwart him from reaching his goals.

In December of 2004, Ibrahim was released as a "low level prisoner."[4] He continued subtle ways of fighting against the US and began the next phase of his plan. He managed to join the Mujahedeen Shura Council in 2006 and became an integral part of the sharia committee that determined how sharia law would be administered to the people of Iraq. He eventually became the general supervisor of Iraq's sharia committee and a member of the senior council that dispensed punishment to people in a sharia court.[5] While presiding over his own sharia court, he became known for his brutality and publicly executed anyone suspected of aiding US led coalition forces. Soon he had complete control of the sharia committee as he succeeded those in power above him. He now had completed the second phase of his plan as he assumed absolute control of the sharia courts in Iraq. His word became a matter of life or death for his countryman through sharia law. He didn't hesitate to administer the harshest punishments to anyone who would oppose him.

It was now time to move on to the third phase of his plan. He had joined al-Qaeda in the fight against the Americans, and now controlled the sharia law courts in Iraq. The third part of his plan would require him to take over leadership of al-Qaeda in Iraq. Ibrahim al-Badri had risen through the

---

4   "U.S. Actions in Iraq Fueled Rise of a Rebel," *The New York Times*, 10 August 2014. Retrieved 23 December 2014.
5   Peter Beaumont, "Abu Bakr al-Baghdadi: The ISIS chief with the ambition to overtake al-Qaeda," *The Guardian*, 1 August 2014. Retrieved 14 June 2014.

ranks of al-Qaeda in Iraq with brutal efficiency until only one man stood in his way. That man was Abu Omar al-Baghdadi, the leader of al-Qaeda in Iraq. Ibrahim waited patiently and gained more and more notoriety until finally one day his opportunity came.

In a joint operation by US and Iraqi forces, the man that stood in his way, Abu Omar al-Baghdadi, was surrounded and killed in a missile attack on April 18th, 2010.[6] The final impediment to Ibrahim's plans was now removed.

Less than a month later, on May 16th, 2010, Ibrahim was named the leader of al-Qaeda in Iraq.[7] The third phase of his plan was now complete. As the new leader of al-Qaeda in Iraq, he wanted to make a powerful statement and orchestrated a series of attacks that were unrelenting in their intensity and brutal in their efficiency in killing others. Anyone that stood against him or questioned his authority was targeted for assassination. Just as Ibrahim was ramping up his campaign of violence in Iraq, something happened that opened the door for him to take over almost all of Iraq. It was an unexpected gift, and he didn't hesitate to take full advantage of this opportunity.

THE WITHDRAWAL OF US FORCES IN IRAQ

This was better than anything Ibrahim could ever have hoped for. The United States withdrew the final remaining ground forces from Iraq in December of 2011. This happened at precisely the time Ibrahim's al-Qaeda forces were rampaging across Iraq. The withdrawal of US forces at this critical time created a power vacuum in Iraq. The

---

6   "Iraqi al-Qaeda leaders killed," BBC News, 19 April 2010.

7   Anthony Shadid, "Iraqi Insurgent Group Names New Leaders," *The New York Times* 16 May 2010. Retrieved 13 June 2014.

Iraqi government forces were not strong enough to hold off al-Qaeda advances, and Ibrahim began a systematic attack of all areas outside government control in Baghdad.

One by one, city after city soon fell to the relentless advance of Ibrahim's al-Qaeda forces. He didn't need to control all of Iraq, just the areas where the oil fields were. The oil fields provided him with nearly unlimited resources and the means to finance his growing army of al-Qaeda warriors. Now flush with vast amounts of money that flowed from the oil fields, nothing stood in his way to achieve the empire he had always envisioned.

With Iraqi government forces weak and vacillating, and confined mainly to the capitol city of Baghdad, Ibrahim announced the further expansion of his vision. He announced the formation of the Islamic State of Iraq and the Levant (ISIL) on April 8th, 2013.[8] This is also known as ISIS. (Islamic State of Iraq and Syria) He moved his forces into Syria to take advantage of the civil war being waged in that nation through the jihadist faction, Jabhat al-Nusra.

At this time, Ibrahim began to distance himself from al-Qaeda in Iraq and all other jihadist factions. He wanted his authority to supersede all other factions and wanted his group to be known as ISIL or ISIS. It was the dream of many Islamic countries to be formed into an Islamic State and Ibrahim had accomplished that goal. Even the name that he chose for his group said that: The **Islamic State** of the Levant. The other portion of the name, the **Levant**, declared what his vision was for this area. The Levant is the area of the Middle East comprised of the nations of Lebanon, Syria, Iraq, Jordan, Palestine, Cyprus, Israel and

---

8   "ISI Confirms That Jabhat Al-Nusra Is Its Extension in Syria, Declares 'Islamic State of Iraq And Al-Sham' As New Name of Merged Group," MEMRI, 8 April 2013. Retrieved 16 June 2014.

the eastern portion of Egypt. Ibrahim wanted to control all areas of the Levant, and now, after his successful expansion into Syria, he wanted something to lend gravitas to the way others viewed him.

In order to accomplish this goal and to prepare the world for the time he would announce the reestablishment of the Caliphate, he knew he had to change his name. He needed to have a name worthy of a caliph. He would be Ibrahim Awad Ibrahim al-Badri no longer. He had to choose a name that would lend authority to him, and yet be a name that would remind people of the Caliphate that they had lost, and the glory that awaited them if they would only unite under his leadership. He searched and finally came up with the perfect name.

ONE NAME TO RULE THEM ALL

The name he chose was **Abu Bakr al-Baghdadi**. Why did he choose this name? To us in the west, this name carries no special significance—yet to those in the Muslim community, it carries great significance. Let's dissect the name he chose to try to gain understanding.

The first part of his new name is Abu Bakr. Who was Abu Bakr and why did he choose this name?

When Muhammad died, the man who was chosen as the first caliph, the one who would run the office of the first Caliphate, was named Abu Bakr. Abu Bakr was the father in law of Muhammad through his daughter Aisha who was married to Muhammad. He was the very first successor of Muhammad.

To Abu Bakr al-Baghdadi, taking the name **Abu Bakr** was brilliant. It was the name of the first caliph, and since he would soon be reestablishing the Caliphate, what better name to be known by than Abu Bakr. This move would be completely in line with Islamic tradition, and history would repeat itself as another Abu Bakr stepped up to establish the Caliphate. He could not ask for a better first part of his name.

The next part of his name was equally as impressive and accurate. He chose **al-Baghdadi**. What was the significance behind this choice of names?

Abu Bakr al-Baghdadi had lived in the city of Baghdad for most of his life. His original surname, al-Badri means "one from Baghdad." Al-Baghdadi was a continuation of identifying himself from Baghdad. But there was a deeper reason that he wanted **al-Baghdadi** as his new last name. The previous golden time of the Islamic Empire had come during the reign of the Abbasid Caliphates. All of the Abbasid Caliphates had ruled from the city of Baghdad, so the al-Baghdadi name brought up a correlation to the Abbasid Dynasty and the best times the Islamic faith had ever experienced.

Now everything was in place. **Abu Bakr al-Baghdadi** was the perfect name and this name conjured up several different associations with previous caliphs. It would lend credence to the time when he would seize control and resurrect the Caliphate once again. But even all this was not enough for Abu Bakr. He had a secret; a secret so powerful that he felt the entire Muslim world would have no choice but to embrace him when he declared the office of the Caliphate was coming back to rule all of Islam again.

Abu Bakr al-Baghdadi's secret was this—he was also a direct descendent of Muhammad through the tenth Imam. To understand the significance of this fact, we need to delve deeper into Islamic history.

As previously stated, when Muhammad died, the majority of the Muslim population choose the strongest leader to govern them and they accomplished this by the formation of the Caliphate. However, there was a portion of Islamic followers that felt only a direct descendent of Muhammad should lead the body of believers. The adherents of this philosophy were the Shia and formed the Shiite branch of Islam. The Shiites comprise about fifteen percent of the Muslim population. They called their successor to Muhammad the "Imam" and there were eleven previous "Imams" that had led the Shiite branch of Muslim believers.

According to Shiite scholars, only a direct descendent of Muhammad through the Imams could lead the Shiite branch of Islam. Abu Bakr was one of the rare ones who was uniquely qualified to be the leader of all Muslim people because he was a powerful leader capable of reinstituting the office of the Caliphate and he was a direct descendent of the tenth Imam. No one else had the qualifications he had. Now it was time to act.

With the success of his ISIS forces in Iraq and Syria, and the proper name chosen, it was now time to make the boldest move anyone in the Muslim world had made in eons of time. It was now time to call the office of the Caliphate back into existence again. The fourth and final phase of his plan had begun.

THE REESTABLISHMENT OF THE CALIPHATE

On June 29th, 2014, the first day of Ramadan, a symbolic and holy day in Islamic tradition, Abu Bakr al-Baghdadi addressed the world and announced the establishment of a worldwide Caliphate.[9] During his audio-taped message, Abu Bakr announced his intentions to establish an Islamic State across all of the Middle East. He also declared his plan to expand into Europe and march on Rome. With visions of previous caliphs in his mind, he said that he would conquer both Rome and Spain; and then he commanded Muslims throughout the world to immigrate to the new Islamic State.[10]

What few people realized on that day, including those of us in the United States, history had just repeated itself in a way that would soon affect everyone in the world. Not only had a man named Abu Bakr stepped forward to reclaim the office of the Caliphate, the office that claimed to speak with one voice for Muslims everywhere, but he had done this almost to the very day when 100 years previously, the seeds of world war were sown on the global stage.

One hundred years before, on June 28th, 1914, Archduke Franz Ferdinand was assassinated setting the stage for a war that would encompass the entire world. Germany emerged as the primary aggressor in two world wars that were fought in the twentieth century.

On June 29th, 2014, one hundred years later, we got a glimpse of who the primary aggressor was going to be in the war of the future. A fanatical Islamic State under the direction of the Caliphate, with Abu Bakr al-Baghdadi as the new caliph, was now the new threat. They had just declared war on Spain, Rome, all of Europe and the rest of the world. The problem was that few people realized

9   Adam Withnall, "Iraq crisis: ISIS changes name and declares its territories a new Islamic state with 'restoration of caliphate' in Middle East," *The Independent* 30 June 2014. Retrieved 30 June 2014.
10   Jessica Elgot, "ISIS Head Abu Bakr al-Baghdadi Warns 'We Will Conquer Rome,'" *The Huffington Post* 2 July 2014. Retrieved 3 July 2014.

what had just happened. The seeds of World War Three had just been sown.

Having the office of the Caliphate dictating Islamic actions is a game-changer. The old, politically correct arguments that Islam is a religion of peace must now be reexamined to see if they are still valid. The new Caliphate under direction of Abu Bakr al-Baghdadi will now declare to the world what Islam is—and the world is clearly not prepared for what it is going to hear.

In an address broadcast to the entire world on May 14th, 2015, Abu Bakr al-Baghdadi said the following:

"O Muslims, Islam was never for a day the religion of peace. Islam is the religion of war." [11]

Abu Bakr meant every word he said in this address. He had just declared war on the rest of the world, and he set his forces on a path to show just how sincere he was when he made this declaration. His actions truly showed that according to the new Caliphate of the Muslim world, Islam was anything but a religion of peace.

Abu Bakr al-Baghdadi shortly after the declaration of the Caliphate.

---

11   Robert Spencer, "Islamic State Caliph: 'Islam Is the Religion of War,'" *Jihad Watch*, May 14, 2015, http://www.jihadwatch.org/2015/05/islamic-state-caliph-islam-is-the-religion-of-war.

CHAPTER THREE
THE NEW ISLAMIC CALIPHATE

What are the implications of the formation of the new Caliphate? What do we need to know to gain proper understanding of this office?

It might be best to examine what the reestablishment of the Caliphate means for the Islamic world first. There is one indisputable fact that no one in the Islamic religion can ignore. The office of the Caliphate was designed to carry on the governance of the Muslim world as an extension of what Muhammad would do. The power and authority bestowed on the office of the Caliphate is absolute. Once the Caliphate is established, it is impossible for the Islamic world to ignore it—regardless of how it came about.

If different Muslim nations don't agree with the new caliph and his direction of the Caliphate, they have the option of meeting together and electing a new caliph. In this manner, a new caliph can be chosen to lead the Caliphate by consensus of the majority of Muslim nations. If they fail to take this action, then the caliph acting as the director of the Caliphate is the new leader of the Islamic world by default. You can try to ignore him if you want, but you will be obligated to follow his direction and orders until he is replaced by someone else. Ignoring the instructions and orders of the new Caliphate just because you may not agree with them is not an option. The leader of the Caliphate has absolute authority and power over the Muslim world. If you do not carry out his orders, you are worthy of death in Islamic tradition.

Abu Bakr al-Baghdadi declared himself the leader of the new Caliphate in June of 2014, and yet the Muslim world has not convened as a body to overturn his claim. The body of Islam has done nothing to dispute his claims and elect a new caliph. Therefore, Abu Bakr al-Baghdadi is now the reigning caliph and his claim to have restored a legitimate Caliphate is valid unless it is overturned by other Sunni Muslim nations. Amazingly, until this point in time, no other Sunni Muslim nation has made this claim. The only thing that we can conclude then, is that Abu Bakr al-Baghdadi is the voice and hand of the Sunni Islamic religion—through the office of the Caliphate. He claims to speak as the single voice for all of Islam. This is a fact that we cannot dismiss or ignore as many people in the political arena are trying to do.

Perhaps this is why we see so much timidity in dealing with Abu Bakr and so few willing to oppose him. We hear loud voices of opposition and dissent, and yet there is no coherent response against him. His reign of terror is increasing and he is recruiting more and more fighters to join the cause of ISIS. He is expanding his influence daily. Yet the leaders of the Western powers keep making excuses for why he is not the face of Islam, and that he is not a true threat to the United States and other nations.

Anyone that claims that the actions of ISIS and the leader of the Caliphate are peaceful hasn't been paying attention. They are also ignoring what Muslim believers know— they are obligated to carry out the orders of the leader of the Caliphate or suffer the consequences. In many cases, Abu Bakr al-Baghdadi has decreed that the penalty for non-compliance is death. This is why you see the deaths of so many Muslim's at his hands. But Abu Bakr hasn't limited his attacks to those under his control in Iraq and Syria. He has expanded his reign of terror all over the world to establish the legitimacy of his worldwide Caliphate.

Here is a list of some of the terrorist attacks orchestrated by ISIS under the direction of the office of the Caliphate through Abu Bakr outside Iraq and Syria.

TERROR ATTACKS BY ISIS THROUGHOUT THE WORLD

Date	Location	Terrorist Event
1. March 22, 2016	Brussels, Belgium	The Brussels Airport and the Maalbeek Metro Station were bombed by five terrorists loyal to the Caliphate of Abu Bakr and ISIS. There were 32 deaths and 300 people injured by Ibrahim El Bakraoui, Najim Laachraoui, and Khalid El Bakraoui and two others. This was the largest terrorist attack ever carried out on Belgium soil.
2. Dec. 2, 2015	San Bernardino, CA	Syed Rizwan Farook and Tashfeen Malik open fire at a holiday party killing 14 people and wounding 22 others. Tashfeen posted on Facebook that they were loyal to the Caliphate of Abu Bakr al-Baghdadi.
3. Nov. 13, 2015	Paris, France	ISIS terrorists loyal to Abu Bakr al-Baghdadi coordinate four attacks in Paris killing 130 people. Countless others were wounded.

4.	Nov. 12, 2015	Lebanon	ISIS suicide bombers conduct two bombings in Lebanon killing 43 people.
5.	Oct. 31, 2015	Egypt	An ISIS affiliate claimed responsibility for bringing down a Russian passenger jet that killed all 224 people aboard the plane.
6.	Oct. 10, 2015	Turkey	Turkish officials linked ISIS to two explosions that killed more than 100 people at a peace rally in the capital of Turkey.
7.	Sept. 24, 2015	Yemen	Two bombs exploded near a mosque during a Muslim holiday and killed at least 25 people. ISIS claimed responsibility for the explosions.
8.	Aug. 7, 2015	Saudi Arabia	A bomb exploded at a mosque and killed 15 people, including 12 Saudi police officers. ISIS claimed responsibility.
9.	July 20, 2015	Turkey	A Turkish man that declared allegiance to Abu Bakr and ISIS killed 32 people at a cultural center.
10.	June 26, 2015	Tunisia	A man linked to ISIS killed 38 people, most of which were British tourists, at a luxury hotel on the beach.
11.	May 22, 2015	Saudi Arabia	An ISIS suicide bomber killed 21 people and wounded 120 others at a Shiite mosque during prayers.
12.	May 3, 2015	Garland, Texas	Nadir Soofi and Elton Simpson, two soldiers of Abu Bakr's Caliphate, opened fire at a "Draw Muhammad" cartoon contest promoting free speech in America.
13.	Apr. 19, 2015	Libya	A video of two ISIS soldiers is released showing them beheading and shooting dozens of Ethiopian Christians.
14.	Mar. 20, 2015	Yemen	More than 130 people at Shiite mosques were killed during prayers by ISIS affiliates.
15.	Feb. 15, 2015	Libya	ISIS warriors loyal to the Caliphate of Abu Bakr line up a group of Egyptian Christians and behead them all.
16.	Jan.7, 2015	Paris, France	Armedy Coulibaly, one of three gunmen that attacked the newspaper Charlie Hedbo, declared allegiance to ISIS and the Caliphate of Abu Bakr al-Baghdadi. 12 people were killed during the attacks.

This is just a partial list of the attacks linked to ISIS and Abu Bakr's Caliphate across the world.[12] This list of attacks, perpetrated by the Caliphate or people loyal to the Caliphate outside Syria and Iraq, accounts for almost 1000 civilian deaths. These people were not armed combatants in the struggle against ISIS; they were everyday people like you or me that were brutally murdered.

Appalling as this list is, it does not account for the atrocities occurring inside Syria and Iraq on a daily basis. This includes the brutal extermination of almost the entire Christian population in this area. According to Eusebius, an early church historian, Christianity had spread to this area through the efforts of the Apostle Thomas when he sent Thaddeus to Mesopotamia to spread the Gospel.

There were hundreds of thousands of Christians in various groups in this area, including the Iraqi Christians, the Syrian Christians, the Yezidi Christians, the Armenian Christians and the Assyrian Christians. Through the atrocities committed by ISIS and other jihadist groups, Christianity, for all intents and purposes, is practically extinct in this area.

The Christians living in Iraq and Syria were the backbone of their communities. They were the small business owners, entrepreneurs, the doctors, the dentists, the lawyers—the ones that made their societies work. They were the ones providing stability to all around them, and provided good jobs to many others in their communities. Yet this did not stop the forces of ISIS and the Caliphate from systematically slaughtering them. Being a Christian in Syria or Iraq is tantamount to having a death sentence placed upon your head. According to the instructions coming from the

---

12   Karen Yourish,, Derek Watkins,, Tom Giratikanon,. "ISIS is Likely Responsible for Nearly 1000 Civilian Deaths Outside Iraq and Syria," *The New York Times* November 17, 2015. Retrieved 23 Nov. 2015.

Caliphate of Abu Bakr al-Baghdadi, you are worthy of death if you are a Christian in his Islamic State.

THE ATROCITIES COMMITTED BY THE CALIPHATE OF ABU BAKR AL—BAGHDADI INSIDE HIS ISLAMIC STATE

It is almost incomprehensible to catalogue the mind-numbing abuses coming from the areas that Abu Bakr controls. His Caliphate has taken man's inhumanity to his fellow man to new extremes. Consider the following things that his minions have done in compliance with his directives:

▶ On Aug. 19th, 2014, American journalist and video reporter James Foley was beheaded by ISIS executioner Jihadi John in Raqqa, Syria. The YouTube video of this event was circulated on the internet and called "A Message to America." James Foley had been captured on Nov. 22nd, 2012 and was killed less than two months after the formation of the Caliphate of Abu Bakr.[13]

▶ On Sept. 2nd, 2014, American-Israeli Journalist Steven Sotloff was shown being beheaded on the internet by Jihadi John in Raqqa, Syria. In August of 2013 Steven Sotloff was kidnapped near Aleppo, Syria and was sentenced to death by Abu Bakr al-Baghdadi despite a plea for mercy from Sotloff's mother.[14]

---

13   Rukmini Callimachi, "Militant Group Says It Killed American Journalist in Syria," *The New York Times,* Aug. 19, 2014. Retrieved Aug. 20, 2014.

14   Michael Wilner, "Islamic state claims murder of Jewish-American journalist in latest beheading video," *Jerusalem Post,* Sept. 2, 2014. Retrieved December 1, 2014.

▶ Royal Jordanian Air Force pilot Muath al-Kasasbeh
was burned alive by ISIS on Jan. 3rd, 2015. His jet
fighter had crashed near Raqqa, Syria on Dec. 24th,
2014 and he was killed after ISIS asked jihadists
on Twitter to propose the method of his death.
A video was released showing him being doused
in gas and then immolated as warriors of the
Caliphate looked on.[15]

▶ On June 26th, 2015, members of ISIS loyal to
Abu Bakr al-Baghdadi threw four homosexual
men off a roof of a building in Raqqa, Syria,
after the Supreme Court of the United States
announced their decision in favor of gay
marriage. The ISIS members used the hash
tag "#Love Wins" on social media to mock the
Supreme Court's decision.[16]

▶ In June of 2015 ISIS placed political prisoners
of the Caliphate into a steel cage and then
slowly immersed them in a swimming pool. The
steel cage containing the victims was lowered
completely in the water and then raised several
times to maximize the terror of the victims
being drowned. Cameras filmed the scene and
then the video was placed on the internet so
the world could see the "infidels" suffering their
horrendous deaths.[17]

▶ Also in June of 2015, more people critical of
the Caliphate of Abu Bakr al-Baghdadi had

---

15   Adam Chandler, "Jordan's King Abdullah Vows Revenge for Death of Mouath
al-Kasasbeh, Who Was Burned Alive by ISIS," *The Atlantic,* February 4, 2015.

16   Michael Lucchese, "ISIS 'Celebrates' SCOTUS Decision by Tossing 4
Accused Gay Men Off Roof," *Brietbart.com,* June 30, 2015

17   Joe Tacopino, "ISIS slowly drowns prisoners in a cage," *New York Post,* http://ny-
post.com/2015/06/24/new-video-shows-isis-slowly-drowning-prisoners-in-a-cage.

explosive wire charges placed around their
necks so video devices could record their
heads being blown off by members of ISIS. The
videos of these gruesome executions were
released on social media sites.[18]

Again, this is just a partial list of the horrific events performed by ISIS at the behest of the Caliphate of Abu Bakr
al-Baghdadi. These events are all documented and verified
by news media outlets. The inhumanly brutal acts being
committed against those in the Christian communities in
the areas controlled by ISIS are so profoundly disturbing
that they almost defy description. Yet that is precisely
what a leader in the Yezidi community tried to do as he
came to the United States. He testified before Congress
on the plight of the Yezidis and other Christians trapped in
the Islamic State.

The man who described the following events before
Congress on December 9th, 2015, was Mirza Ismail, chairman of the Yezidi Human Rights Organization-International.
The events he testified about before our Congressional
leaders were not wild exaggerations or hear-say accounts,
but the actual testimonies from those in his community
that had suffered at the hands of ISIS and the office of the
Caliphate administered by Abu Bakr al-Baghdadi. When he
finished his description of the things that had befallen the
Yezidi community, the Congressional leaders were stunned
and shocked into silence.

---

18   Sharona Schwartz, "Islamic State's Latest Execution Video May Be Its
Most Horrifying Yet," *TheBlaze*, June 23, 2015, http://www.theblaze.com/sto-
ries/2015/06/23/islamic-state-groups-latest-video-of-executions-may-be-its-
worst-yet.

A YEZIDI LEADER TESTIFIES BEFORE CONGRESS

Mizra Ismail, the chairman of the Yezidi Human Rights Organization-International told Congress, "Because we are not Muslims, and because our path is the path of peace... **we are being burned alive.**" He then went on to describe other acts being committed by ISIS.

"There are thousands of young Yezidi women, girls, and even children, who as I speak, have been enslaved and forced into sexual slavery. These girls are subjected to daily, multiple rapes by ISIS monsters," Ismail testified before the Congressional audience. He then expanded upon his comments.

"According to many escaped women and girls whom I talked to in Northern Iraq, the abducted Yezidis, mostly women and children, number over 7,000. Some of those women and girls have had to watch 7-, 8-, and 9-year old children bleed to death before their eyes, after being raped by ISIS militia multiple times a day."

He continued on, "I met mothers, whose children were torn from them by ISIS. These same mothers came to plead for the return of their children, only to be informed, that they, the mothers, **had been fed the flesh of their own children by ISIS.** Children murdered, then fed to their own mothers."

Mizra Ismail's account was still not finished. "ISIS militia have burned many Yezidi girls alive for refusing to convert and marry ISIS men. Young Yezidi boys are being trained to be jihadists and suicide bombers. All of our temples in the ISIS controlled area are exploded and destroyed."

According to Mr. Ismail, the tragedy started when ISIS militia infiltrated the Yezidi controlled area in Sinjar on August 3rd, 2014 and began the extermination of the entire Christian population. The men are systematically slaughtered, leaving the women and children to suffer at the hands of ISIS if they could not escape.

Mizra Ismail concluded his remarks before Congress by saying, "What I have just recounted to you, what has happened to the Yezidis and Chaldo-Assyrian Christians and other minorities in Sinjar and in the Nineveh Plain is nothing less than genocide, according to the UN definition."[19]

Mr. Ismail is absolutely right. Christians are suffering genocide at the hands of ISIS and the Caliphate of Abu Bakr al-Baghdadi. What is remarkable is that the world is surprisingly nonchalant and unwilling to face the realities presented by the Islamic State under the direction of the Caliphate. Our political leaders insist we follow the mantra of political correctness and say that Islam is a religion of peace. They do not see and fail to recognize what is happening on the world stage right under their noses. They begrudgingly acknowledge horrific acts of terror, and then dismiss them as if these acts were some sort of aberration and not the belief system of Muslims who are loyal to the Caliphate.

Islam may be a religion of peace to some in the Muslim community, but to millions of others who have fallen under the hypnotic spell of Abu Bakr's instructions as the mouthpiece of the Caliphate; Islam is anything but a religion of peace. As Abu Bakr has declared, Islam is a religion of war. Its terrorism and conquest will not be stopped until we acknowledge this fact and deal with it. Millions upon millions of Islamic people following the directives of the new Caliphate *do* recognize the horrendous acts described here

---

19   Zachary Leshin, "Yezidi Leader Tells Congress: 'Because We Are Not Muslims...We Are Being Burned Alive,'" *cnsnews*.com, December 11, 2015, http://www.cnsnews.com/news/article/zachary-leshin/congressional-testimony-because-we-are-not-muslims-we-are-being-burned-alive.

as being characteristic of Islam; and they are fighting a religious war to prove it. They cite chapter and verse from the Quran to justify their actions, and are willing to kill anyone who would say otherwise, including other Muslims.

We are in a war to the death with the warriors of the Caliphate, and the only ones that do not seem to realize this fact yet is us.

THERE IS A BETTER WAY

After reading the depressing list of atrocities committed by ISIS and the Caliphate, it might help to reflect on the words of the Apostle Paul in his first letter to the Corinthians. He placed everything in proper perspective when he made the following comments:

> If I speak in the tongues of men and of angels, but have not love, I am only a resounding gong or a clanging symbol. If I have the gift of prophecy and can fathom all mysteries and all knowledge, and if I have a faith that can move mountains, but have not love, I am nothing. If I give all I possess to the poor and surrender my body to the flames, but have not love, I gain nothing. Love is patient, love is kind. It does not envy, it does not boast, it is not proud. It is not rude, it is not self-seeking, it is not easily angered, it keeps no record of wrongs. Love does not delight in evil but rejoices with the truth. It always protects, always trusts, always hopes, always perseveres. Love never fails. (1 Corinthians 13:1-8 NIV)

CHAPTER FOUR
THE IMPLICATIONS OF THE RENEWED CALIPHATE FOR OTHER MUSLIM POWERS

To gain more understanding of the situation in the Middle East, it might be helpful to see what other Muslim powers think of ISIS and the renewed Caliphate. What are their unique perspectives in regard to Abu Bakr al-Baghdadi? Is he well accepted or are there serious reservations about his claim to be the leader of the Caliphate? Let's take a look at some of the major players in this region starting with other Sunni nations and ending with the Shiite nation of Iran.

TURKEY'S HISTORY WITH THE CALIPHATE

Let's start with the nation of Turkey, a country with considerable clout and history in regard to the office of the Caliphate. Turkey, a Sunni nation, once dominated the entire region of the Middle East through the auspice of the Ottoman Empire. The Ottoman Empire was a major world empire that dominated large portions of the globe including much of Southeastern Europe, the Middle East and Northeastern Africa from 1300 through the year 1918.

It's impossible to review the history of Turkey and not acknowledge the fact that Turkey was the home of the Muslim Caliphate for almost 500 years. It began when the first Islamic Caliphate of Mehmed II captured the city of Constantinople in 1453. From that period on, the institution of the Caliphate remained in Turkey, the home of the Ottoman Empire, until its downfall in 1918.

What led to the downfall of this long standing empire? After all, they had been through numerous wars and upheavals for centuries and had always managed to survive. Was there any key event that happened that contributed to the disintegration of their empire?

It's true that Turkey had aligned itself with Germany in WWI, and while that was a contributing factor, there is another crucial event that has often been overlooked in history that was critical to the disintegration of the Ottoman Empire. It was an insidious event that is scarcely acknowledged to this day and barely talked about in world history. The event I am talking about was the first example of "genocide" in the modern world.

This tragedy began on April 24th, 1915 when the government of Turkey and the religious office of the Caliphate declared jihad on the Armenian Christian population living in their land. The Armenian Christians had formed the first independent Christian nation in the world with millions of people living in their country for centuries until they were absorbed by the Ottoman Empire. Then on April 24th, 1915, Turkey's government decided this peaceful Christian group was a threat to their nation and systematically rounded up all the Christian leaders and intellectuals and killed them.

The Ottomans began a campaign of extermination that targeted every Christian they could find. Some Armenian Christians were herded into the mountains and killed, while others were forced to march into the deserts on endless walks without food or water until they died. When this holocaust ended, over one and a half million Armenian Christians had lost their lives.[20]

The Ottoman Empire had endured for centuries until they committed this unspeakably brutal act against the Christian population living within their borders. Less than three years after their campaign to eliminate all Christians living among them, the Ottoman Empire crumbled and untold numbers of their citizens lost their lives as the ravages of WWI continued. When the fog of war finally cleared, the vast empire that had once controlled huge portions of the world was no more. What was left the world carved up to define new national borders where the once mighty Ottoman Empire had stood.

This was accomplished through the Sykes-Picot Agreement of 1916. This plan created the new nations and boundaries we are familiar with today in the Middle East from the former ruins of the Ottoman Empire.

The institution of the Caliphate managed to hold on a few more years in Turkey after the First World War ended until the last official caliph, Abdulmecid II, was deposed by Turkey's leader Mustafa Kemal Ataturk on March 3rd, 1924.[21]

The nation of Turkey had a history that was intertwined with the office of the Caliphate for almost 500 years. They do not take that history lightly. The Caliphate was

---

20   Glenn Beck, *It Is About Islam* (New York, NY: Threshold Editions/Mercury Radio Arts, 2015), P. 53.
21   Wikipedia, "The Ottoman Caliphate," last revised 28 March, 2015, http://en.wikipedia.org/w/index.php?title_Ottoman_Caliphate&oldid=653919004.

synonymous with Turkey when it was a world empire, and the leadership from the Caliphate was integral to the success it enjoyed at that time. To Muslims, one of the darkest days in Islamic history occurred when the Caliphate was dissolved in 1924. To the body of Muslim believers, the loss of the voice of Islam through the Caliphate was an inconsolable loss. They no longer had a united voice leading them. The Muslim world fell into disarray and chaos and began to squabble and war with each other. This was not the way it was supposed to be and Turkey was partially to blame because they were the ones that abolished the Caliphate.

MODERN DAY TURKEY AND THE CALIPHATE

Particularly conscious of the vacuum created by the loss of the Caliphate, the present-day President of Turkey, Recep Tayyip Erdogan, took notice as Abu Bakr al-Baghdadi reinstated the office of the Caliphate on June 29th, 2014. He was astonished and furious as he witnessed the unmitigated gall of al-Baghdadi when he declared the office of the Caliphate into existence once again. In the eyes of the President of Turkey, this pretender to the throne did not have the authority to do as he had just done. It takes a united voice of the entire Muslim world to reinstitute the office of the Caliphate, and al-Baghdadi had just done it alone proclaiming himself as the new caliph. This could not stand, and Erdogan, the President of Turkey, was determined to do something to return the office of the Caliphate to its rightful place.

The Caliphate must be returned to Turkey, its proper place in the eyes of Erdogan. After all, Turkey controlled the Caliphate for centuries, and it was only in Turkey that the legitimate caliph could dominate the world once again. But how was Erdogan going to make this happen? There is a problem with any hasty action to delegitimize Abu Bakr al-Baghdadi, because in the process he could be calling into question the very legitimacy of the office of the Caliphate. No—the Caliphate must be preserved and at some point in the future it will be seized and returned to Turkey. This is the quandary facing the President of Turkey.

So far, Recep Tayyip Erdogan, the President of Turkey has played a waiting game with ISIS and Abu Bakr al-Baghdadi. This strategy has worked to his advantage because everyday ISIS seems to be making more enemies. Every time they kill more and more Muslims and enrage other nations in the world, the case is strengthened to return the office of the Caliphate to Turkey—the more modern and tolerant nation. Abu Bakr al-Baghdadi is playing right into the hand of Erdogan with each atrocity committed. The President of Turkey is patiently waiting for the day when Abu Bakr will go too far—and commit an act of war so egregious that other nations will be forced to act against him. When that time comes, the nation of Turkey will be ready to step in and take over the office of the Caliphate again. Until then, it is a waiting game that Erdogan seems to be winning.

THE BIBLICAL PERSPECTIVE ON TURKEY

There is a biblical perspective that Turkey is fulfilling whether they realize it or not. In their quest for world dominion as leader of the Caliphate, they are fulfilling a scenario that was written about in the Bible thousands of years ago. The Bible speaks of a coalition of nations led by an enigmatic leader called Gog that arises from a power base centered in the nation of Turkey. (This will be described in detail later). If at some point the nation of Turkey is able to seize control of the office of the Caliphate, it would fulfill the description of the power base from Turkey that controls and directs the actions of other nations as they rise to fulfill one of the most cataclysmic battle scenes presented on the pages of the Old Testament. How this happens will be explained in a later chapter.

THE SAUDI ARABIAN VIEW ON THE CALIPHATE

Saudi Arabia has emerged as the richest and most influential member of the Muslim nations in the Middle East. How did this come about? What are their views on the Caliphate and the history surrounding the rule of the Caliphate in this region? In order to answer these questions, we need to review the history of the Saudis.

Saudi Arabia is home of "Wahhabism," a branch of Islam that believes that the Muslim faith has been contaminated through the years by the influences of the outside world. This belief system arose from the teachings of Muhammad ibn Abdul Wahhab, a Sunni cleric born in 1703. He taught that Islam had strayed from their pure faith by being corrupted by superstition and the influences of Christians and Jews. He founded the "**Salafist**" branch of Islam that taught that the Muslim religion needed to get back to the purer form of Islam practiced by the early ancestors and followers of the prophet Muhammad. In fact, the word "Salaf" means "ancestor" in Arabic.

In order to spread his teachings and have more influence, Wahhab formed an alliance with the powerful Saudi tribe in the central Arabian Desert. They gathered an army and fought to promote their purer form of Islam. They were repulsed by the leadership coming from the Caliphate that was centered in the Ottoman Empire in Turkey. To the followers of the Salafist movement, the Ottoman Caliphates had degenerated into corrupt old men that were mostly concerned with amassing wealth and harems of beautiful women. They felt that the Muslim religion deserved better, and they were constantly at odds with Turkey and the Ottoman Empire.

As World War I began, Britain was thwarted in their early plans for dominion in Turkey as the disastrous Battle of Gallipoli was fought. The British troops and their allies failed to dislodge the Ottomans from their stronghold in Turkey. The allied nations regrouped and developed a different plan to take advantage of the enmity between the Saudis and the Ottoman Empire. Britain appointed an opportunistic young leader named T.E. Lawrence to foment a rebellion against the Ottomans with Lawrence in league with the Saudis and another powerful Arabian tribe called the Hashemites. T.E. Lawrence was better known as "Lawrence of Arabia." Because of his dashing leadership, and the might of the Saudi and Hashemite armies supporting him, Lawrence of Arabia was able to defeat the Ottomans and seize control over much of the Middle East. This enabled the nations of the world to set up the current boundaries of the nations in this area we see today after WWI.

One of the critical events that happened near the end of World War I was the proclamation of a land to be set aside for the Jewish people. This was accomplished by the "Balfour Declaration" of 1917 when the British government promised the Jewish people access to their former ancestral homeland. Without the collapse of the Ottoman Empire, this event could have never taken place.

The modern day kingdom of Saudi Arabia arose from the ruins of the vanquished Ottoman Empire and today remains the home of the Salafist version of Islam. They became the richest of the Muslim nations with the discovery of oil in the 1930s, which they developed with the help of the Standard Oil Company. The revenue from their oil ventures has allowed the Saudis to expand their influence over the entire Middle East.

Another thing that has enabled Saudi Arabia to extend its influence is the fact that they control the Islamic holy sites of Mecca and Medina. The city of Mecca is the location of the Kaaba—the epicenter of the hajj pilgrimage that every Muslim believer is required to take. The Kaaba is a shrine adorned in purple and scarlet coverings and covered with gold and precious stones. The door of the elaborate shrine is made of pure gold. Inside this shrine where the Muslims come to worship is a black meteorite stone that is said to be a representation of Allah. There is a tremendous amount of symbolism in the Islamic religion associated with this structure and this is the location that all faithful Islamic believers kneel and pray toward during their prayers.

In a later chapter we will talk more of this site in Mecca because, with careful examination of the Scriptures, this shrine in Mecca holds far more significance than we could imagine and is critical in our discussion of end-time events.

Muslim believers surrounding the Kaaba, the Islamic Holy Shrine in Mecca

CURRENT DAY SAUDI ARABIA'S VIEW OF THE RENEWED CALIPHATE

Saudi Arabia has a new king leading the country. His name is King Salman bin Abdulaziz Al Saud—or better known as King Salman. He was appointed as king of Saudi Arabia on January 23rd, 2015 and is believed to be eighty-one years old.

King Salman has made it clear that he will tolerate no outside intervention in his country; and this includes any meddling from ISIS or any directives coming from the renewed Caliphate of Abu Bakr al-Baghdadi. It would seem that the Salafist views of Saudi Arabia and the Caliphate of Abu Bakr would mesh since al-Baghdadi traces his lineage back to one of the early ancestors of the prophet through the tenth Imam. This however, is not the case. King Salman sees Abu Bakr as a clear threat to the stability of the region and wants nothing to do with the new leader of the Caliphate.

The new leader of Saudi Arabia has enough headaches already with the tragedies surrounding the deaths of 2400 Muslims in the crush of the crowds during the hajj pilgrimage during September of 2015 according to an independent Associated Press tally.[22] When you add the tensions generated by the execution of 47 people convicted of terrorism on January 2nd, 2016—including a prominent Shiite cleric from Iran named Nimr al-Nimr; then you have more drama than the new ruler ever wanted in the first year of his reign. There are not only tensions with the new Caliphate, but increasing troubles with Iran who is emerging as a new threat on the world stage with the implementation of the Iranian Nuclear Deal. All in all, the situation in Saudi Arabia is in transition and is uneasy at the current time—in fact many describe the future of this powerful kingdom as "bleak" with dark times awaiting them.

THE IRANIAN VIEW OF THE CALIPHATE

The other major player in the Middle East is the nation of Iran. Iran is a proud country and the former home of the Persian Empire that dominated much of the Middle East after Cyrus the Great conquered the city of Babylon in 550 BC. Their empire lasted until they were conquered by Alexander the Great. Iran was once a decisive force on the world stage and they wish to regain some of their former glory.

The problem facing Iran is that they are a Shiite Muslim nation; and that places them in direct opposition to the Sunni Muslim nations of Turkey and Saudi Arabia. The Shiite Muslims comprise only about fifteen per cent of body of Islamic believers—and Shiites have always viewed

---

22   Aya Batrawy, "Decisive Saudi king marks first year on throne," *Spokesman Review*, 24 January 2015, p. 3.

themselves as a persecuted minority in the world of Islam. That's because the Shiites believe that the only proper leadership of Islam comes from a direct descendent of Muhammad, and was represented by a series of "Imams" that lived in previous ages.

The Shiite view is that there have been a series of twelve Imams that arose to guide the Islamic faith after the death of Muhammad. Eleven of the twelve Imams were killed by the direct orders of the Sunni Muslims through the office of the Caliphate—the opposing leadership option in Islam that thinks only the strongest leader should speak as the voice of all Muslim believers. Because eleven of the previous Imams were eliminated by the ruling office of the Caliphate in their time, the Shiites believe they have been unjustly persecuted. They await the time when the "12th Imam" returns to lead the entire Muslim nation after a series of catastrophic defeats rock the Islamic world.

This may seem like an odd viewpoint but it is the firm belief system of the Shiite Muslims in Iran. After eleven of the former Imams were killed by the Caliphate, the Twelfth Imam went into occultation (hiding) in the year 872 AD, and has promised to return to lead the Islamic world in the aftermath of their worst defeat. (This will be described in detail later.)

To summarize, Iran has an entirely different viewpoint on who should be leading the body of Islam. They have always been at odds with the Caliphate, and that remains true to this day. They absolutely detest the leadership of Abu Bakr al-Baghdadi, and have actively fought against ISIS and the newly reinstated Caliphate. They want Abu Bakr al-Baghdadi defeated, and in their eyes, anything they can do to bring about this defeat will hasten the return of the promised "Twelfth Imam." This creates a truly volatile situation in the Middle East.

When you add the new reality of the Iranian Nuclear Deal with the United States, Iran has emerged as a prominent new power player in the Middle East, and their new power could be far more destabilizing to the area of the Middle East than we could ever have imagined.

THE PRESENT REALITIES OF THE RENEWED CALIPHATE

This is the setting in which we now find ourselves. Instead of unifying the Muslim world, the resurrection of the Caliphate has created a deep divide and renewed profound enmities between the powerful Muslim nations. ISIS is raging out of control and is trying to provoke other Muslim nations into a confrontation because they won't follow their leadership. Turkey hates Abu Bakr and is patiently waiting until they can take over the office of the Caliphate. The Saudis see the new Caliphate as a threat and want nothing to do with ISIS. The Iranians want the Caliphate and ISIS destroyed in a catastrophic fashion to usher in the revealing of the Twelfth Imam.

Into this boiling pot of agendas and twists and counterplots steps Abu Bakr al Baghdadi as the mouthpiece of the Caliphate. He is moving forward with his plans despite what the rest of the Muslim world thinks about him. With ISIS carrying out his decrees, Abu Bakr has a reason why he is carrying out every horrendous act and atrocity. His reasons will be the topic of the next chapter.

CHAPTER FIVE
COUNTDOWN TO A SHOWDOWN

To nearly everyone in the world, the actions of ISIS and the renewed Caliphate administered by Abu Bakr al-Baghdadi seem almost suicidal. What could be motivating them? Why are they taking the actions they are and demanding that the rest of the Muslim world follow them? What is ISIS hoping to accomplish?

To answer these questions, we need to look at some of the most recent actions of ISIS, and see if we can find some underlying clues that will give us insight into what they are thinking. Perhaps then we can find the motivation behind the heartless actions of ISIS.

THE RELEASE OF A GRUESOME VIDEO

On November 16, 2014, ISIS released a video showing a man in orange prison garb on his knees with his head shaved. The man was an American aid worker named Peter Kassig.

Standing over him was a man clad in black and speaking with a British accent. He looked directly into the camera and spoke the following words:

> To Obama, the dog of Rome: today we are slaughtering the soldiers of Bashar and tomorrow we will be slaughtering your soldiers. Soon we will be slaughtering your people on your streets... The spark of this conflict was lit in Iraq, and its heat will continue to intensify by Allah's permission until it burns the crusader army in Dabiq. And here we are, burying the first crusader in Dabiq; eagerly awaiting for the remainder of your armies to arrive.[23]

Shortly after the rants of the man in black subsided, Peter Kassig was decapitated along with others in the video. As his blood stained the sands of the desert, what few failed to realize is the location where these murders were carried out. It happened in Dabiq, a small town in the northwestern corner of Syria. If we are to understand the significance of this, we need to learn more about the importance of Dabiq in Islamic prophesy.

THE PROPHECY OF DABIQ

Dabiq may seem like an insignificant town in Northern Syria, but it is the location of one of the most famous prophesies of Muhammad according to commentaries on the prophet's words.

---

23 "Gruesome Islamic State Video Announces Death of Peter Kassig," *The Clarion Project*, November 16, 2014, http://www.clarionproject.org/news/gruesome-islamic-state-video-announces-death-peter-kassig.

Dabiq is the place where the Muslim version of Armageddon will take place. The prophecy of Dabiq is the only known predictive prophecy ever given by Muhammad. In Dabiq, the forces of Islam will triumph over the forces of Rome in a decisive end-times battle. It will open a pathway into Europe where Islamic forces will eventually triumph over the Vatican. While this may sound absurd when you first hear it, there is far more to this than you may realize. Before we get into that, let's take a look at the prophecy of Dabiq so we know exactly what it predicts.

> The Last Hour would not come until the Romans would land at al-Amaq or in Dabiq. An army consisting of the best (soldiers) of the people of the earth at that time will come from Medina (to counteract them)...They will then fight and a third of the army would run away, whom Allah will never forgive. A third which would be constituted of excellent martyrs in Allah's eye would be killed and the third who would never be put to trial would win and they would be conquerors of Constantinople. (Muhammad, according to Hadith)

In other words, according to Muhammad, there is an end-time battle coming where Islamic forces will annihilate the forces of Rome in their version of Armageddon. The "Romans" are viewed by ISIS and Abu Bakr as any coalition forces fighting against Islam including the United States. ISIS is so enthralled with this prophesy that they even named their magazine "Dabiq" after the name of the location where the Muslim forces will triumph. This is the battle that ISIS wants and the battle that ISIS hopes will draw the forces of Rome into Dabiq. This is their goal: to lure the armies of the world to Dabiq where they will be destroyed.

The actions of Abu Bakr al-Baghdadi seem to indicate that he envisions himself as the Islamic leader that leads this decisive victory at Dabiq. His ISIS forces are acting under his direction to force this confrontation into reality. Abu Bakr wants the armies of the world and Rome to become so enraged by the actions of ISIS that they literally send their armies to Dabiq where Bakr believes they will be annihilated. And Abu Bakr thinks he is just the leader to accomplish this task.

THE MOTIVATION OF ISIS AND THE CALIPHATE OF ABU BAKR AL—BAGHDADI

Abu Bakr al-Baghdadi wants to force the battle of Dabiq to take place so Islamic armies can triumph over western armies. Everything he does has this purpose in mind. He has the battle of Dabiq foremost on his mind when he directs ISIS to commit atrocities and murder. He has told his followers that they can make this battle come to pass if they will only follow his direction. Abu Bakr wants foreign armies to come to Dabiq to fight him—this is the reason for the following actions:

- ▶ The attacks on Paris, France on November 13th, 2015 that resulted in the deaths of 130 French citizens were carried out to provoke France to send an army to fight ISIS.

- ▶ The genocide of Yezidi Christians and other Christians in Syria and Iraq was carried out to force the armies of Christian nations to come to Dabiq to fight ISIS where Abu Bakr thinks they will be destroyed.

- ▶ James Foley, Steven Sotloff and Peter Kassig were all decapitated on video to provoke the United States to resend ground forces to the conflict with ISIS in Iraq with hopes that these ground forces will expand into Syria also where they will be killed in Dabiq.

- ▶ On the cover of ISIS's digital magazine called Dabiq, a picture was posted showing the flag of ISIS flying over the Vatican in Rome. This was done to provoke Romans to come to Dabiq to fight ISIS.

This is just a partial list of the things Abu Bakr has done to provoke the end-times confrontation of Dabiq. While he may be convinced that he is the leader to make all of this come to pass, perhaps we should review some details that may call into question the veracity of his claims. Let's do a reality check on what Abu Bakr has actually accomplished as a leader of the Caliphate.

THE REALITY OF ABU BAKR AL—BAGHDADI'S CALIPHATE

The main thing Abu Bakr has been able to accomplish is to turn the world against him—including the Islamic countries. The nation of Turkey and their President Recep Tayyip Erdogan can't stand Abu Bakr. They want him destroyed and anything that can be done to accomplish the demise of al-Baghdadi would be beneficial to Turkey. If the new caliph was destroyed, then the office of the Caliphate could be moved back to Turkey where the Turkish people think it rightly belongs. Until that time, Abu Bakr al-Baghdadi will be tolerated, and if he can be undermined and ISIS destroyed, then all the better for the nation of Turkey.

The nation of Saudi Arabia wants Abu Bakr eliminated and the threat of ISIS removed. The new Caliphate under al-Baghdadi is a threat to the security of the region, and threatens the Saudi's profits from oil revenues and their lucrative control of the cities of Mecca and Medina. They know that Abu Bakr wants to control these Muslim Holy Sites and they will do everything in their power to prevent that from happening. They will lose their power and prestige if Abu Bakr al-Baghdadi succeeds in his quest to control all Sunni Muslims through the office of the Caliphate. Saudi power is slipping in this region because of plummeting oil prices and this makes the threat of Abu Bakr even greater. Anything that can be done to remove the menace of Abu Bakr would be viewed positively by Saudi Arabia.

Iran is actively fighting against ISIS and the new Caliphate through their proxies like Hezbollah in Lebanon. The renewed Caliphate is a direct threat to their vision of the "Twelfth Imam" coming back to lead all Muslim believers. The office of the ancient Caliphate killed the eleven previous Imams, and Iran is determined to prevent that from happening again. They want Abu Bakr al-Baghdadi destroyed and the Caliphate along with him—and the more cataclysmic way this can be accomplished the better. The Shiites of Iran believe that the only way their future leader, the Twelfth Imam, will come out of hiding is by the catastrophic defeat of Islamic armies according to their prophecies. If these Muslim armies just happen to be led by the Caliphate—then this is a double victory. The tremendous defeat of other Muslims led by the Caliphate will bring forth their promised Imam and removed the competing power structure in Islam at the same time. This is the exact scenario that Iran is looking for.

The nation of Iran was given a tremendous opportunity to accomplish this exact scenario recently. With the Iranian Nuclear deal concluded in January of 2016, Iran has been infused with 150 billion dollars of capital from the United States. Does anyone really think that one of the greatest terrorist nations in the world will not use this tremendous stockpile of cash to force their vision of world dominion into reality? We will discuss how they will do this in a later chapter.

ABU BAKR'S INCORRECT INTERPRETATION

President Obama was referred to as the "dog of Rome" in the video released showing the killing of Peter Kassig. While this was meant to be a derogatory term to President Obama, it also implied that the President was carrying on an agenda set forth from the Vatican and that the President was under the control of Pope Francis. Is this a correct interpretation of what President Obama has been doing?

There isn't the slightest shred of evidence that would support this conclusion. The President has met the Pope in America only once, and this meeting was a cordial exchange of world leaders. It is ludicrous to say that the President is following instructions given by the Pope. Furthermore, the military forces of the United States have never been characterized as the "armies of Rome" or "Roman." In fact, at this point in time, no army in the world can be characterized as a Roman army with the exception of the small Italian army.

There is a way however, through a particular set of circumstances, that an army can be formed that will be known as a "Roman" army. This will be discussed in detail in a later chapter.

It would appear that the ruler of the new Caliphate, Abu Bakr al-Baghdadi has gotten many things wrong. Not only is he calling the armies of the world by the wrong name, but he erred in his perceptions of how the Muslim world would receive him. He thought the other Sunni Muslim nations would embrace him, and he thought Iran would welcome him with open arms because of his ancestry and lineage with the Tenth Imam. When others disagreed with him, he began his murderous spree of killing all that opposed him. It didn't matter if they were Muslims, Christians or Jews. In Abu Bakr's eyes, you are worthy of death if you don't carry out every word and whim coming out of his Caliphate.

In spite of all of this, his most egregious error is when he actively opposed God. It's not enough in Abu Bakr al-Baghdadi's eyes to just oppose his fellow men—now he is purposefully campaigning against the God of Abraham, Isaac and Jacob. This is his greatest error and a mistake from which he will never recover. Let's take a look at how he is ensuring his own destruction and the fate that awaits him.

CHAPTER SIX
THE FATE OF ISIS AND ABU BAKR AL—BAGHDADI

Besides the crimes detailed in previous chapters, what else did Abu Bakr al-Baghdadi and his followers in ISIS do that guarantees a humiliating fate unless they immediately change their actions? They have directly gone against what our Heavenly Father has declared for the nation of Israel. When you directly go against the Will of God, then you place yourself in a very precarious position.

Perhaps this will clarify things. Abu Bakr has decreed that the area of the "Levant" belongs to ISIS. So there can be no question as to what they mean, here is a map of the Levant and the territories ISIS says belongs to them:

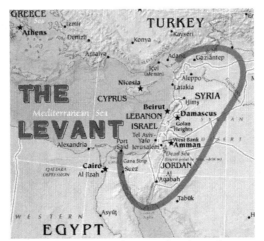

ISIS map of the Levant—the area they intend to control

In the viewpoint of ISIS, the Levant includes the nations of Lebanon, Syria and Jordan, and parts of Iraq and Egypt. In the heart of the Levant lies the nation of Israel. The Caliphate of Abu Bakr and his minions in ISIS will not stop until they control the entire area of the Levant—and therein lies the problem.

God has said that the area of the Levant belongs to the nation of Israel. He said that unequivocally in Genesis:

> In the same day the Lord made a covenant with Abram, saying, "Unto thy seed have I given this land, from the river of Egypt unto the great river, the river Euphrates." (Genesis 15:18)

The area of the Levant belongs to the nation of Israel. So there can be no questions, here is a map depicting the land grant to Israel from the Lord:

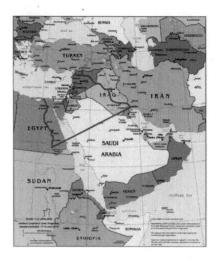

As you can see from the area indicated on the map, the land area granted to Israel by the Lord looks remarkably similar to the area claimed by ISIS. Our Heavenly Father's land grant to Israel includes the modern day nations of Israel, Lebanon and Jordan, most of Syria, and portions of Iraq, Saudi Arabia, and Egypt.

You can practically superimpose the maps of the Levant claimed by ISIS and the land grant given to the nation of Israel in Genesis chapter fifteen. These two maps represent the different destinies envisioned for this area. One is the vision of ISIS and the Caliphate of Abu Bakr al-Baghdadi, and the other is the vision of the Lord for His people Israel as outlined in His Word. Which of these competing visions will win out in this disputed area?

The answer was given almost three thousand years ago. It is found in the pages of the Bible in a place that few would look for it. The answer can be found in Psalm 83. While most of us think of the Psalms as a place where we can find praise and worship for the Lord, it is also a place where we find a description of a war. The sweeping description in

Psalm 83 describes a conflict that ultimately leads to the borders of a modern day Israel that God envisioned for his people. Just how does this war accomplish this feat? To find that answer we need to carefully examine what Psalm 83 is telling us.

THE PSALM 83 WAR

The details of the Psalm 83 war were given by an unlikely source. They were provided by someone that most of us would not think of as a prophet. He was a musician and a prophet in the royal courts of King David and wrote several of the Psalms. His name was Asaph and he wrote specifically about our day and time when he spoke of Israel in Psalm 83. The precision and insight with which he speaks could have been taken from today's headlines instead of being written several millennia ago. Here is what he said:

> O God, do not keep silent; be not quiet, O God, be not still. See how your enemies are astir, how your foes rear their heads. With cunning they conspire against your people; they plot against those you cherish. Come, they say, let us destroy them as a nation, that the name of Israel be remembered no more. (Psalm 83:1-4 NIV)

The common mantra of ISIS and the Caliphate of Abu Bakr al-Baghdadi is that Israel has no right to exist and should be destroyed as a nation. Asaph's words from so long ago are a modern day reflection of what ISIS has said and what many Muslim nations are saying today about the contemporary nation of Israel. Asaph then goes on to list the nations in the Psalm 83 coalition:

> With one mind they plot together; they form
> an alliance against you—the tents of Edom,
> and the Ishmaelites, of Moab and the Hagrites,
> Gebal, Ammon and Amalek, Philistia, with the
> people of Tyre. Even Assyria has joined them
> to lend strength to the descendants of Lot.
> (Psalm 83:5-8 NIV)

To most of us today, this list of names in the coalition that have plotted against Israel is almost indiscernible. Keep in mind that one of our goals in gaining understanding what is going on in the Bible was to look at things with a Middle Eastern perspective. We don't understand and recognize these names and the areas that they represent because we don't live in the lands the Bible is talking about. One thing that works to our advantage is the fact that the Bible has listed these people and modern scholars have identified where they live. We don't have to guess who they are or the nations where they are located. Here is a list of the nations where these people currently reside.

THE NATIONS AND PEOPLE OF PSALM 83:

- ▶ Edom-Esau: located in Southern Jordan

- ▶ Ishmaelites: Saudi Arabians

- ▶ Moab: Central Jordanians

- ▶ Hagrites: Egypt

- ▶ Gebal: Northern Lebanon

- ▶ Ammon: Northern Jordanians

- ▶ Amalek: Arabians south of the Dead Sea and Northeastern Egypt

- ▶ Philistia: Palestinians of the Gaza Strip and West Bank

- ▶ Tyre: Lebanon

- ▶ Assyria: Syria and portions of Iraq

- ▶ Descendants of Lot: Moab and Ammon—Jordanians

If we were to look on a map, we would discover that these are the nations that currently surround Israel. You have Lebanon, Syria and Iraq to the North of Israel, Jordan to the East, Saudi Arabia to the Southeast, and Egypt to the West of Israel. The tiny nation of Israel is surrounded on all sides by nations that want to destroy them.

What is interesting in the description of the Psalm 83 coalition of nations is the fact that this coalition has been "given strength" by Assyria which we now know to be the nation of Syria and parts of Iraq. This is exactly where we find ISIS operating today. The power base of the Caliphate of Abu Bakr is in Syria and Iraq. Dabiq is in Syria and Raqqa, the place where the power structure of the Caliphate and Isis resides, is in Syria also.

What is even more startling is the fact that ISIS has officially declared provinces—or wilayat—in Egypt and Saudi Arabia where ISIS has a firm infrastructure and many followers.[24] It seems that ISIS is strengthening its hold over the entire area and expanding wherever it can. Even the areas surrounding Israel that ISIS does not currently control—namely Lebanon, Jordan and Palestine—have all been involved in three major wars and have tried to eradicate the nation of Israel from the map. Each has been condemned in the Bible for trying to destroy the nation of Israel and told that continued aggression against the Jewish State will result in their destruction. Israel is surrounded by a legacy of hatred, with ISIS emerging as the major player in the power structure arrayed against the Jewish nation.

THE FATE OF THE PSALM 83 NATIONS

What does the Psalm 83 prophesy say will happen to the coalition of nations that come against Israel? The prophet Asaph said that they are going to "perish in disgrace," and elaborates giving the following details:

> Make them like tumbleweed, O my God, like chaff
> before the wind. As fire consumes the forest or
> a flame sets the mountains ablaze, so pursue
> them with your tempest and terrify them with
> your storm. (Psalm 83:13-15 NIV)

These nations that come against Israel are going to be destroyed. They are going to be like chaff or tumbleweeds that are consumed by a fire. In fact, the fate of each of

---

24   Karen Yourish, Derek Watkins, Tom Giratikanon, "ISIS is Likely Responsible for Nearly 1000 Civilian Deaths Outside Iraq and Syria." *The New York Tims,* Nov. 17, 2015. Retrieved 23 Nov. 2015.

these nations is given in detail in different areas of the Bible. The nation of Jordan is going to suffer extensively from the aftermath of the Psalm 83 war. Jordan contains three of the groups named in Psalm 83, Edom, Ammon and Moab. Here is what the Bible says about these three groups of people:

> This is what the Sovereign Lord says: Because Edom [Jordan] took revenge on the house of Judah and became very guilty by doing so, therefore this is what the Sovereign Lord says: I will stretch out my hand against Edom and kill its men and their animals. I will lay it waste, and from Teman [Jordan] to Dedan [Saudi Arabia] they will fall by the sword. I will take vengeance on Edom *by the hand of my people Israel*, and they will deal with Edom in accordance with my anger and my wrath; they will know my vengeance, declares the Sovereign Lord. (Ezekiel 25:12-14 NIV) (Italics mine)

The nation of Jordan is going to be "laid waste." We also received an important clue in this verse on how the destruction is going to be accomplished. It says: "By the hand of my people Israel." The people of Israel are the ones that are going to be carrying out this destruction. The Israeli army is called the "Israeli Defense Forces" or IDF and from this Scripture we learn that they are the ones carrying out the destruction that will befall the nation of Jordan.

Ammon and Moab are located in Jordan too and the Bible says that Ammon will be "wiped out from among the nations and exterminated from the countries." (Ezekiel 25:7 NIV) The fate of Moab in Jordan is no less severe. The

Moabites will "not be remembered among the nations, and I will inflict punishment on Moab. (Ezekiel 25:10, 11 NIV)

The nation of Jordan is going to suffer extensively from their involvement in the Psalm 83 War—and the defensive forces of Israel, the IDF, are the ones that are going to be carrying out this destruction. What about the other nations involved in this fight? What is their fate according to the Bible?

The city of Tyre in Lebanon is going to be "destroyed and left without house or harbor." (Isaiah 23:1 NIV) Tyre is currently a stronghold of Hezbollah, a Shiite faction fighting against Israel.

Philistia, the Palestinians, "will be destroyed and none will be left, and Gaza will be abandoned." (Zephaniah 2:4-5 NIV) The Palestinians currently occupy the Gaza strip and the West Bank area near Jerusalem.

Egypt will suffer when "the land of Judah will bring terror to the Egyptians." (Isaiah 19:17 NIV) Egypt will lose land in this war and five Jewish cities will be set up in former Egyptian lands. One of these cities will be called the "City of Destruction." (Isaiah 19:18 NIV)

Saudi Arabia is going to be warned to turn and flee if they do not want to suffer the same destruction that comes on the nation of Jordan. "Turn and flee, hide in deep caves, you who live in Dedan, [Northern Saudi Arabia] for I will bring disaster on Esau [Jordan] at the time I punish him." (Jeremiah 49:8 NIV) Northern Saudi Arabia is included in the land grant given to the nation of Israel in Genesis. If Saudi Arabia fights in this war, the Northern portions of their country will be destroyed just as Jordan will be destroyed. Saudi Arabia has the option of withdrawing their forces south from Dedan to prevent losses in this war. It is up to them.

What will be the fate of ISIS and Syria in this war? They currently occupy land in Syria and parts of Iraq. One of the most hotly contested areas in Syria right now is the city of Damascus. Damascus is currently held by the forces of Bashar al-Assad, the President of Syria, who is actively fighting against ISIS. He is being assisted by Vladimir Putin and his Russian forces. It is a tenuous battle with both sides struggling to gain complete control of Syria. Each side has had gains and losses, with neither side able to dislodge the other.

In the Psalm 83 war scenario, the most tragic fate awaits the Assyrians [Syria]. ISIS is firmly in control of many areas in Syria except the areas around Damascus. God's Word describes something absolutely terrifying that happens to these nations fighting against His people. "A fire consumes the forest or a flame sets the mountains ablaze." (Psalm 83:14 NIV) The effects are seen most clearly in the city of Damascus. The city of Damascus is going to be annihilated and will become a heap of ruins. We are told this is the book of Isaiah:

> An oracle concerning Damascus: See, Damascus will no longer be a city but will become a heap of ruins. (Isaiah 17:1 NIV)

Damascus is going to be so thoroughly destroyed that there will hardly be anything recognizable left in what remains of the city. There will be complete devastation where the longest continually inhabited city in the world once stood. Little will be left.

If there is any question that the destruction of Damascus is related to the war described in Psalm 83, then the following should place any doubts at rest. The chapter in Isaiah describing the horrendous fate of Damascus uses the same key words that we find in the Psalm 83 prophesies. Psalm 83 describes the fate of the aggressors against Israel in the following manner: "Make them like *tumbleweed*, O my God, like *chaff* before the wind." (Psalm 83:13 NIV) The Isaiah 17 chapter uses the exact same words in the description of the devastation that awaits the Syrians in Damascus or any people that stand against the Lord. "Although the peoples roar like the roar of surging waters, when he rebukes them they flee far away, driven before the wind like *chaff* of the hills, like *tumbleweed* before a gale. In the evening, sudden terror! Before the morning, they are gone!" (Isaiah 17:13-14 NIV)

The words "chaff" and "tumbleweed" are both used in the descriptions of the destruction that will take place. This imagery ties both of these passages together. From the description in Isaiah, we also get a clue on how long it takes this destruction to occur. The passage in Isaiah says that the terror leading to devastation begins in the evening, and by morning the destruction is accomplished. "In the evening, sudden terror! Before the morning, they are gone!" (Isaiah 17:14 NIV)

What could cause something like this to happen? How exactly is the destruction detailed in Psalm 83 and the other passages we have just reviewed going to take place? While we are not given the exact means how this devastation is accomplished, we are provided several crucial details that may allow us to make an educated guess on how this occurs. Let's list the salient details.

CLUES ON HOW THE PSALM 83 WAR IS ACCOMPLISHED

- ► The nations affected by the destruction are the immediate neighbors of the modern day nation of Israel. (Psalm 83)

- ► The nation of Jordan is going to be set on fire and burned like stubble until they are laid waste. (Obadiah 1:18; Ezekiel 25:13)

- ► Lebanon (Tyre) will be laid waste so that there is no house left. (Isaiah 23:1)

- ► Palestine will be destroyed so that no inhabitants are left. (Zephaniah 2:5)

- ► Northern Saudi Arabia (Dedan) will be laid waste. (Ezekiel 25:13)

- ► Damascus in Syria is going to be a ruinous heap. (Isaiah 17:1)

- ► The destruction of the Psalm 83 coalition of nations is going to be carried out "by the hand of my people Israel." (Ezekiel 25:14) This means the Israeli Defense Forces or IDF.

- ► The method employed for the destruction will cause the areas affected to burn up like chaff and tumbleweed, and will consume the forest with fire and set the mountains ablaze. (Psalm 83:13-14)

- ► The destruction will start in the evening, and will be finished by morning. (Isaiah 17:14) When the devastation of this war starts, it will be accomplished very rapidly and will end in less than twelve hours.

Given all the clues from the description of the Psalm 83 war, and the fact that many areas will be laid waste, that the IDF will be the ones causing the destruction, that the forests and mountains will be set on fire, and that all of this devastation will occur in less than twelve hours; then I think it is safe to conclude that nuclear weapons are involved. Nuclear weapons are the only weapons currently in the arsenal of man that can cause the type of widespread devastation described in these passages.

The question then becomes...Does the nation of Israel possess nuclear weapons?

ISRAEL AND NUCLEAR WEAPONS

One of the worst kept secrets in the Middle East is that the nation of Israel has nuclear weapons in its arsenal. If the Caliphate of Abu Bakr al-Baghdadi manages to unite the Muslim nations surrounding Israel long enough to coordinate an attack—then the Psalm 83 coalition of nations becomes an immediate reality and an attack against Israel is certainly within the realm of possibility. If this attack happens and the Caliphate of Abu Bakr uses any atomic, biological or chemical weapons, then the attacking nations can expect a swift and predetermined response from Israel. If the nation of Israel is ever threatened with complete and total annihilation, it has said many times that it will exercise the Samson Option.

What is the Samson Option? The name is based on the biblical character Samson, who when faced with certain death at the hands of the Philistines who were holding him captive, chose to use his tremendous strength to bring down the temple of Dagon by pushing down the pillars holding the temple up. The result was the death of thousands of his enemies even though he himself was killed. The Samson Option that Israel has developed involves the use of nuclear weapons in its possession. When Israel is threatened by overwhelming military force, to the point where its survival is in jeopardy, it reserves the right to use nuclear weapons to defend itself.

Experts estimate that Israel has between 70 to 200 nuclear weapons in its possession.[25] The capabilities of their arsenal are as varied as the arsenal itself. While they have nuclear weapons capable of destroying huge swaths of land in the multiple kiloton variety, they in all likelihood have weapons of limited nuclear capacity as well. These limited nuclear weapons will restrict the size and scope of the damage done. This includes suitcase sized nuclear devices and neutron bombs, which can be launched by aircraft or rockets. Neutron Bombs kill by using enhanced radiation, but do little damage to the surrounding infrastructure and the radiation effects dissipate rapidly. These weapons would permit surgical strikes against an enemy bent of the destruction of Israel.

There is little ambiguity that Israel has nuclear weapons. The description of events in Psalm 83 certainly sounds like the description of nuclear weapons being used. If this is correct, then there are two questions of paramount importance. When is the Psalm 83 War going to happen? Does the Bible give us any clues? And secondly, what would cause Israel to use such drastic measures and deploy the Samson Option? That will be the next topic of our discussion.

---

25   Robert S Norris, et al, "Israel Nuclear Forces, 2002," Bulletin of the Atomic Scientists, September-October 2002, (excerpt) 58 (5): 73-75, doI10.2968/058005020.

CHAPTER SEVEN
THE BIBLICAL PRECEDENT FOR THE TIMING OF THE PSALM 83 WAR

Does the Bible give us any clues about when we can expect the pivotal Psalm 83 War to happen, or are we left in the dark with the details being so obscure that they are unfathomable to the average person? While we have not been given any specific date that we can expect these events to occur, perhaps we can look at other events that have happened recently to see if we can find any clues to the time frame the Bible provides. One of the best ways to do that is to look at Jewish history.

If we are going to garnish any clues from Jewish history, then perhaps we should start with one of the most momentous events that paved the way for the restoration of the Jewish people to their home land. For centuries, the Jewish homeland and the city of Jerusalem had been controlled by Muslim forces. Most recently (1917) it was controlled by the Muslim Caliphate and the distinctly Islamic Ottoman Empire. The Turkish Ottoman forces controlled the area around Jerusalem with such a tight fist that they said they would never relinquish control of Jerusalem. In fact, they said that it was impossible for them to ever give up control of Jerusalem. To prove just how impossible it would be for them to ever leave Jerusalem, they developed a saying that implied the impossibility of ever overthrowing their dominion over this area. They said:

> When the waters of the Nile flow into Palestine, then will a prophet of the Lord come and drive the Turks out of this land.[26]

The Turks were doubly sure they would never leave Jerusalem because it was impossible for the Nile River to flow miles and miles across the Sinai Desert into Palestine, and all the prophets of God had ceased thousands of years ago. This saying had been true for countless centuries, and the Turks were convinced that the sword of Islam would always hold sway over the area around Jerusalem.

THE IMPOSSIBLE HAPPENS

A man was sent by British forces to free the Jewish home-land and the city of Jerusalem from Islamic domination in World War I. His name was General Edmund Allenby and he was placed in charge of British, Australian and New Zealand armed forces. On October 31st, 1917, he put his plan for the recapture of the city of Jerusalem into action. One of the problems plaguing his troops was the lack of water in this area. To solve this problem, General Allenby had his engineers tap into the Nile River and run a

---

26 Into All Truth, "As Birds Flying: Jerusalem 1917," Into All Truth Ministries, http://www.nccg.org/iat/birds.html.

pipeline that followed the advance of his troops right into Palestine. His troops had access to thousands of gallons of water a day that came directly from the Nile River. When General Allenby and his troops reached the gates of Jerusalem, he had his airplanes drop leaflets telling the Turkish Muslim forces inside Jerusalem that if they left immediately they would not be fired upon. Miraculously all Turkish troops fled the city the night of December 8th, 1917, and by December 9th they were all gone. In a period of forty days, General Allenby had accomplished the impossible and captured the city of Jerusalem without a shot being fired inside the gates of Jerusalem.

General Allenby walks into Jerusalem through the Jaffa Gate
(Gate of the Friend)

When Turkish forces were questioned about their frantic departure from Jerusalem, it became apparent that they were absolutely terrified of General Allenby. In Arabic, the name Allenby translates into Allah-en-Nebi which means "Prophet of God." To the Turkish Muslims, a man named the prophet of God brought the waters of the Nile into Palestine and ended an occupation that had lasted many centuries. They left because an impossible prophecy had been fulfilled.

The method General Allenby used to clear the city of Jerusalem from the Ottomans was a fulfillment of prophecy. He had his planes flying over the city dropping leaflets with strict orders not to fire a shot or cause any damage to the city of Jerusalem. In Isaiah, we read the following:

> Like birds hovering overhead, the Lord Almighty will shield Jerusalem; He will shield it and deliver it, He will pass over it and will rescue it. (Isaiah 31:5 NIV)

This was just the beginning of many biblical precedents that were fulfilled as Israel began the task of moving back into their ancestral homeland. December 9th, the very day the last of the Islamic troops left the city was a special day of blessing for Jerusalem. In Jewish history at the time of Haggai the prophet, a group of Jews had been sent back to Jerusalem to rebuild the temple. After many false starts and distractions that impeded their progress, on the very day they began their task of rebuilding the temple, a special blessing was placed on that date and the city of Jerusalem by the prophet Haggai. That date fell on the 24th day of the ninth month—it was a special day and a day that the Jews were told to "consider" three times in that Scripture. (Haggai 2:15-18) The ninth month is called Kislev in the Hebrew calendar, and the 24th day in the month of Kislev in 1917 just happened to fall on December 9th of that year. That was the very day the last of the Turkish troops fled Jerusalem. They left on a special day of blessing for the city of Jerusalem.

THE JUBILEE YEAR

Just as the land was cleared for the return of the Jewish people, there is another precedent that may provide some important insights on the timing on the complete return of the Jewish homeland to the nation of Israel. It is found in the commandment to observe the Jubilee years. What exactly are the Jubilee years?

In Leviticus, the ancient nation of Israel was told that every seventh year was a sacred year, or Shemitah year, and they were given special instructions on how to live their lives during that year. After seven of these Shemitah years, or a period of forty-nine years, the fiftieth year was to be consecrated as a special year to the Jewish people. This fiftieth year was known as the "Jubilee" year and this special year was set apart for liberty and the restoration of family and ancestral lands. We find this in Leviticus:

> Count off seven Sabbaths of years—seven times seven years—so that the seven Sabbaths of years amount to a period of forty-nine years. Then have the trumpet sounded everywhere on the tenth day of the seventh month; on the Day of Atonement sound the trumpet throughout your land. Consecrate the fiftieth year and proclaim liberty throughout the land to all its inhabitants. It shall be a jubilee for you; each one of

> you is to return to the family property and each
> to his own clan. The fiftieth year shall be a jubi-
> lee for you...In this Year of Jubilee everyone is to
> return to his own property. (Leviticus 25:8-13)

The restoration of ancestral lands was an integral part of the Jubilee year. This precedent was set up when the children of Israel entered the land of Canaan—a land set apart for the house of Israel by the land grant given to them in Genesis 15:18. Since that time a Jubilee year has occurred after every forty-nine years at the start of the fiftieth year. Jewish scholars have pointed out that the year 1917 was a Jubilee year—a year set aside for the return of ancestral lands. It is absolutely incredible that the exact year General Allenby freed Jerusalem and paved the way for Jewish people to reoccupy their land occurred on a year that the Lord set aside for this exact purpose. This was the 68th Jubilee year for the house of Israel and the Jewish people began the slow migration back to the land of their ancestors on that date.

Does the pattern of the Jubilee year, where the Jewish people regained control of more of their ancestral homelands, hold true for the next Jubilee year that started fifty years later? That would place us in the year 1967. What happened in 1967?

The nation of Israel was reborn on May 15th, 1948 after an intense struggle with the Muslim nations surrounding them in their War of Independence. While they had regained some of their ancestral homelands, Muslim forces had regained control of the city of Jerusalem—it was firmly in the hands of Islamic forces.

Something happened in 1967 that changed all this. In June of 1967, the nation of Israel had noted significant preparation by the army of Egypt to launch an all-out offensive against their tiny nation. Israel launched a pre-emptive strike to prevent this catastrophic attack. Israel soon found itself standing against the combined armies of the nations of Egypt, Syria, Jordan and Iraq.

In what can only be described as a miracle, Israel prevailed against overwhelming odds and defeated the combined armies of the nations trying to destroy them. They accomplished this feat in just six days from June 5th through June 10th of 1967. With this victory, the Jewish people regained control of Jerusalem and a significant amount of land they had controlled in ancient times including the Golan Heights, the West Bank, the Gaza strip and the Sinai peninsula.

What is most remarkable is that the feat of regaining control of more of their former homeland just happened to occur during another Jubilee year. The Jubilee year was a time for the return of ancestral homelands and in the sixty-ninth Jubilee year in 1967 that is exactly what happened yet again.

THE 70TH JUBILEE YEAR

The 70th Jubilee Year promises to be a Jubilee year with the most profound significance yet. There are several reasons why this is true. Let's list these reasons so we can have a better understanding of just what we are all facing.

▶ The nation of Israel is still not in control of all of the land they were granted as a nation in Genesis. Here is their promise: "To your descendants I give this land, from the river of Egypt [Nile River] to the great river, the Euphrates." (Genesis 15:18) The part of their land grant they are lacking at this point in time includes areas in Lebanon, Palestine, Syria and Jordan, and parts of Saudi Arabia and Egypt. Curiously enough, those are the exact areas described in detail in the Psalm 83 war. This would imply there is a coming conflict on the horizon where the nation of Israel is going to go to war with these nations and as a result of this conflict; Israel will gain control of all of the land that the Lord has specifically given them. This will greatly increase the borders of the tiny nation we know as Israel today.

▶ ISIS and the Caliphate of Abu Bakr al-Baghdadi have laid claim on the Levant and said this is an area that Islam should control. Their land claim for the Levant and an Islamic State is exactly the same area the Lord has said belongs to the nation of Israel. ISIS is trying to incite a war in this area by unleashing a torrent of terrorist events in the Levant and other areas of the world. They are trying to force an Islamic prophecy to come to pass where they believe they will triumph over Roman forces that come to do battle in a place called Dabiq in Syria.

▶ Untold millions of people have been displaced from Syria and Iraq by the actions of ISIS and the Islamic Caliphate. Anyone who does not agree with Abu Bakr al-Baghdadi is subject to death including other Muslims, Christians and Jews. This has been broadcast in videos and by social media sites throughout the world. Should a major war break out in this area, millions will have been saved because they have fled these countries.

▶ ISIS and the Islamic Caliphate are at war with the forces of Bashar Assad. President Vladimir Putin has come to the aid of President Assad with his Russian forces to further complicate matters in Syria. Neither side is able to gain the upper hand at this point in time.

This is currently the situation on the ground in the Middle East. To further press the point, the 70th Jubilee year has already begun in Israel. It began on Yom Kippur in 2015, which fell on September 23rd, 2015. The 70th Jubilee year lasts through October 12th, 2016. Is there any special significance to the fact that this is the 70th Jubilee year?

The number seventy has special significance in the Bible. It represents the number of completion or fulfillment. The prophet Daniel spoke of 70 sevens that were determined upon the people of Israel until their redemption will come and fulfillment will happen. (Daniel 9:24) Jeremiah spoke of 70 years of judgment that came against Israel because they did not keep the Sabbath years. (Jeremiah 25:11) When Peter came to Jesus and asked him how many times he should forgive his brother he was told not just seven times—but 70 times seven. (Matthew 18:22)

The 70th Jubilee year is no ordinary Jubilee year. I believe it's a mega or super-Jubilee year. Could this year represent the complete culmination of the Lord's plan for the house of Israel—the penultimate destiny for the nation set apart by the Hand of God? I believe every other Jubilee year has been leading to this 70th Jubilee year—when the people of

Israel see the fulfillment of the promise made to them and the complete return of the entire land area set aside for Israel. If this is true, the promise of the 70th Jubilee year means that we are going to start seeing some profound changes in the area of the Promised Land.

We have seen what happened when the 68th Jubilee year took place—the way was prepared for the Jewish people to occupy their homeland once again. The 69th Jubilee year saw the city of Jerusalem returned to the house of Israel after a six-day war. Our own normalcy bias may prevent us from being prepared for what may happen during this 70th Jubilee year and beyond. We may think there are going to be a few changes—but the promises made to the entire house of Israel could mean sweeping changes are in store for the entire area of the Middle East. If this is the case, Israel will no longer be the tiny nation fighting for a foothold in the area where Jesus once walked—it will be a superpower with boundaries that were set apart for their nation thousands of years ago by the Hand of God.

There is something else absolutely fascinating about this 70th Jubilee cycle that is too astounding to be purely co-incidental. It has to do with King David and the length of his reign over the united kingdom of Israel in ancient times. King David ruled for 7½ years in Hebron and 33 years in Jerusalem for a total of 40½ years. We are told that in the following Scripture: "David was thirty years old when he became king, and he reigned forty years. In Hebron he reigned over Judah seven years and six months, and in Jerusalem he reigned over all Israel and Judah thirty-three years." (2 Samuel 5:5 NIV) What is absolutely astounding is that David was a type of Jesus, and David's throne was given to Jesus after He arose into Heaven. Jesus has been sitting on the throne of God since His death. Jesus died in the middle of a Jubilee cycle and has been sitting at the right hand of the throne of God for 40½ Jubilee cycles. Here is the fascinating part: David reigned as King on the earth for 40½ years, Jesus has reigned as King in Heaven for 40½ Jubilee cycles. And right now the 70th Jubilee cycle, the cycle that heralds completion or fulfillment, is just beginning. Should we be taking notice?

The things that may soon happen represent the complete fulfillment and manifestation of the perfect Will of God. Should we expect any less from the onset of the 70th Jubilee cycle? If the pattern we have mentioned above is correct, then the 70th Jubilee year should usher in some of the most intense changes the world has ever seen. That doesn't mean we should be date setting—because that is up to the Will of God and His perfect timing. It does imply however that we should be paying special attention to the things going on around us in this critical time frame. Things could start getting very interesting during the Jubilee cycle of 2016 and the completion of the 70th Jubilee year in October of 2016—or they may not...it is up to God.

If the 70th Jubilee year does reflect completion or fulfillment, then we must prepare ourselves for some pretty challenging times in our future. Just when these things will happen we do not know, rather we should be prepared at all times for anything coming upon us. It would seem that we might expect another major war in the Middle East and all the uncertainty and turmoil that comes along with it. Just how that may come about is the topic of our next chapter.

CHAPTER EIGHT
THE EVENT THAT SETS THE WORLD ON FIRE

There are moments in history that seem to stand apart from all others—when our world changes forever and we are caught up in the drama unfolding all around us. Certainly the events surrounding 9/11 were one of those times. Everyone remembers what they were doing on that day and where they were when they saw the Twin Trade Towers plunging toward the ground. The events of that momentous day left an indelible scar on all of the United States.

The event that is going to happen in the future will have the same impact—only this time it will be felt by the entire world. Something is going to happen that will catch the world by surprise and will forever alter the course of global history. What is this event? What could possibly have such an impact that it will cause the people of the world to stop in their tracks and take notice?

Before that event is described, let's set the stage for the onset of this incident. In our discussion so far we have described many different perspectives and beliefs about what is going to happen in the future. Each perspective seems to be valid and based on things written in each belief system. However, there is one big problem at the current time. Many of these sayings seem to be at odds with each other. They don't jive and fit together with current circumstances in the world.

For example: the forces of ISIS and the Caliphate of Abu Bakr al-Baghdadi want to provoke a "Roman" army to come to a small town in Syria called Dabiq where they will be destroyed in the Islamic version of Armageddon. The problem is that there is no army currently operating in the world's armed forces that is called a "Roman" army. ISIS may call the armed forces of the United States and other western forces a "Roman" army, but that is an incorrect characterization. They have never been under any direct leadership coming out of Rome.

Another problem is the existing state of affairs in the nation of Israel. The Jewish people are satisfied with the borders of their nation as they are currently constituted. There is no push by Israel to gobble up vast new tracts of land promised in ancient times that are presently occupied by other countries. Prime Minister Benjamin Netanyahu has never exhibited any characteristics that would even suggest such a move. He has however staunchly insisted that he will defend the nation of Israel from any enemies and anyone who tries to attack their tiny nation or threatens their existence. Prime Minister Netanyahu will not let that happen and will use any means at his disposal to accomplish this protection.

Complicating matters further, the entire area of the Middle East has been destabilized with the deal the United States made with Iran on their nuclear weapons. Iran is a Shiite nation that represents only about fifteen per cent of the total Muslim population. This radical portion of the Islamic population now has vast torrents of money raining down on them from their lucrative arms deal with the US. What is worse is the fact that Iran hates the Caliphate and will do anything in their power to eliminate the office of the Caliphate from the earth. They have two reasons for doing this. First, the office of the Caliphate killed all of the previous Imams whom the Iranians insist should lead all of Islam. The Iranians see the Caliphate as a direct threat to their chosen leader who will soon come out of hiding to lead the entire Muslim world. Secondly, there are Islamic prophecies that say the hidden leader; the "Twelfth Imam" will only emerge from hiding after the Islamic World has suffered a tremendous defeat. Anything that Iran can do to hasten the defeat of other Muslims and the office of the Caliphate will be viewed as a way to bring about the fulfillment of this prophecy. In their view, the Twelfth Imam will lead them to worldwide dominion.

Also it is important to note that while Iran may not currently be in possession of a nuclear weapon because of the nuclear treaty with the United States, it certainly has the means to procure one from other nations that are known to possess nuclear capabilities. This includes the nations of North Korea and Pakistan. Both of these nations are suffering economically and the huge infusion of cash bestowed upon Iran from the nuclear deal may be too tempting for Iran to ignore. If they can't build one, they can certainly buy one from either of these other two countries. Once they have nuclear weapons, nothing will stand in the way for Iran to accomplish the vision it has for itself and the future leader that will come out of hiding to lead the Muslim world. That has not happened yet and all that is required is the destruction of other Islamic forces to bring it to pass.

This places Iran in a far more prominent position than they have ever experienced in eons of time.

The nation of Turkey wants the Caliphate of Abu Bakr al-Baghdadi destroyed. The President of Turkey Recep Tayyip Erdogan sees the upstart caliph as a pretender to the throne of the Caliphate and an illegitimate leader of Islam. He must be destroyed so the office of the Caliphate can move back to Turkey. The problem is that Turkey cannot move against the office of the Caliphate without delegitimizing the office. An outright attack against ISIS and Abu Bakr by Turkey is unthinkable, and yet a way must be found to destroy ISIS and Abu Bakr without Turkey being implicated. Then Turkey can swoop in and reclaim the office of the Caliphate and control the Muslim world just like the Ottoman Empire used to control all of Islam. But how can they accomplish this feat?

These are the problems facing the various countries in the Middle East. There are different viewpoints and different Islamic prophecies that seem to work against each other to prevent the fulfillment of any them. **There is one scenario however that can make each of the different prophecies and viewpoints fit together like a glove, and can place in motion a series of events that will bring to pass every prophecy and viewpoint that we have discussed so far.** The problem is it will make everyone who hears it cringe and hope that it never occurs. As painful as it may be, let's discuss that particular scenario.

ALL ROADS LEAD TO ONE CONCLUSION

There is one way that everything can be set in motion that will bring about the disparate philosophies coalescing in a coherent manner. It is absolutely tragic but almost inescapable. It also unlocks a series of biblical prophecies that foretell what the future has in store for this area. The event that causes everything to be set into motion is the following:

At some point in time, ISIS and the Caliphate of Abu Bakr al-Baghdadi are going to use an atomic weapon against their enemies. The use of nuclear weapons will unleash a series of reprisals and counter-responses that will set end-time events into motion.

This may seem like a bold statement but consider the following. In May of 2015, The Times of Israel reported in its English-language magazine that ISIS claimed that a nuclear attack by ISIS jihadists on the United States was "infinitely more possible today" than it was a year ago.[27] This was not considered an idle threat by the government of the United States. In response to this threat, the US military began "Operation Jade Helm," which mobilized military forces across the US as an exercise to respond to a nuclear attack against our country. The Operation started in the summer months of 2015 and lasted until September.

ISIS threatened the United States and even proposed the way they were going to accomplish an attack on our country. They said that they could easily procure nuclear weapons from corrupt weapons dealers that had access to either Pakistan or North Korea. Then it would be a rather simple procedure to smuggle these weapons across the relatively unprotected southern border of the United States. Whether this scenario is pure fantasy or a sincere threat against our nation, it brings up the rather startling state of vulnerability that faces the US. We have failed

27   Times of Israel Staff, "IS claims it is 'infinitely' closer to nuking US," *The Times of Israel*, May 24, 2015, http://www.timesofisrael.com/is-claims-infinitely-greater-chance-of-nuking-us/?utm_campaign=cca690d8.

to protect ourselves from a terrorist organization that is bent on our destruction. In fact, many of our highest public officials seem totally oblivious to this real threat against our country. They would rather deal with the challenge of "climate change" than the real threat posed by a tyrannical madman determined to procure a nuclear weapon and use it against us.

Is a nuclear attack against the United States a real possibility? The people and institutions charged with the defense of our nation seem to think that it is a real possibility. The threat level that predicts the possibility of attack against our country has been raised to the highest level and has stayed elevated throughout 2015 and into 2016. There is a palpable tension in the air that has not diminished since the summer months of 2015 and seems to be increasing even now. People seem to be on edge and anxiety levels are increasing. Intolerance for others and over-the-top reactions to the slightest provocations have greatly increased. You only have to look at the racial tensions that have been exploding across the nation in 2015 as verification of this troubled state so prevalent in our country.

The stock market seems to be manifesting the overall mood of the country. It is almost schizophrenic in the wild gyrations happening on a weekly basis. Wild fluctuations of 200 to 300 points a day are now almost routine in their frequency. The slightest hint of bad news sends the stock market tumbling. People are greatly concerned that the stock market could plunge by 50% yet again and wipe out the promise of retirement and the value of their 401k investments. Uncertainty is plaguing the markets.

No one knows for certain if the United States is going to be hit with a nuclear weapon by terrorist groups determined to bring about our downfall. It would be foolish of us not to consider this a real threat. We dismissed even the possibility of something like this happening before and then we were hit by the events of 9/11. Now those opposed to us want to bring about something even bigger than 9/11. What is most problematic is the fact that they have the means to accomplish this feat, they have the determination to make this attack a reality, and they have the people willing to carry out these suicide missions with a zeal unencumbered with moral ambiguities. They think they will be rewarded for our deaths—a viewpoint that is totally foreign to most rational people. On top of all this, they have telegraphed their plans to us in advance and almost dared us to try to stop them.

This is the reality of the threat facing the United States today. Will a nuclear attack happen on US soil? No one knows for sure. It has been 70 years (there's that number again) since a nuclear weapon has been used on another country. The nation was Japan, and in August of 1945 two nuclear weapons were dropped on the cities of Hiroshima and Nagasaki. The nuclear weapons were deployed by the United States in an effort to end World War II. Since that time nuclear weapons have never been used against another country.

If nuclear weapons were ever used again, there would be a profound change in the thinking of all mankind. The nuclear genie would be out of the bottle—and instead of considering these weapons as "doomsday" devices that would lead to the end of the world, nuclear weapons would be considered as practical weapons that could achieve measurable results in tactical situations. The human toll would be ignored in the pursuit of achieving military victories that may not be able to be achieved by any other means. Many of the newer nuclear devices are limited in the scope and damage they do. Some use enhanced radiation (Neutron Bomb) that quickly dissipates after usage, while others limit the scope of damage to a restricted area (suitcase nukes).

If a terrorist group like ISIS ever got their hands on a nuclear device, does anyone even doubt that they would use it as quickly as possible? They want to provoke a war, in fact the fulfillment of their Armageddon scenario at Dabiq depends on the fact that other nations are so enraged by their actions that they come to Syria to destroy them. The use of a nuclear weapon would practically guarantee that event would happen. The eyes of the world would be focused on the Middle East and particularly on Syria. Everyone would be watching events unfold in Syria.

While an attack on the United States or even other areas of the world are a possibility, the area of a nuclear attack that would prompt the response seen in the Psalm 83 war is most likely in or near the nation of Israel. How would something like that happen?

THE MIDDLE EASTERN ATTACK SCENARIO

While we can't know for sure how an attack in the Middle East might occur, we can certainly make an educated guess base on all the facts we have. The following scenario is definitely within the realm of possibility.

The nation of Iran, flush with the cash doled out to them from the Nuclear Treaty with the United States, is able to procure nuclear weapons from either Pakistan or North Korea. Iran knows that if they were to use these weapons then they would be at risk of having their nation destroyed by a nuclear response from the United States or Israel. They don't want that to happen—but there is another way to accomplish their goals without placing their country at risk. They allow these nuclear weapons to make it into the hands of ISIS and the Caliphate of Abu Bakr through a circuitous route of subterfuge while maintaining complete deniability. ISIS is manipulated into receiving these weapons. Iran knows that ISIS will use these nuclear devices. This in turn will be a tremendous victory for Iran because they know that the use of nuclear devices will lead to the destruction of anyone foolish enough to use them. Iran suspects that ISIS and the Caliphate of Abu Bakr al-Baghdadi will be destroyed in response by the nation against which they deploy the nuclear device.

True to form and because of the cult of death surrounding them, ISIS and their new caliph wade into this quagmire of deceit oblivious to the fact that they are being manipulated. Abu Bakr through the mouthpiece of the Caliphate declares jihad or holy war against the nation of Israel. He calls on all Sunni nations to attack Israel and says that Syria will be leading the attack on the Jewish nation. He guarantees success in their attack against the nation of Israel (he has the nuclear device as the guarantee for success) and calls on all the countries that have fought wars against Israel in the past to join him. This includes the nations of Lebanon, Jordan, Egypt and the Palestinians.

While these countries do not necessarily follow the dictates of the new Caliphate, they see an opportunity to rid the world of the nation of Israel. All of these nations were involved in the three major wars against the Jewish state in the past and once again decide to participate in an effort to erase the nation of Israel from the Levant. They all attack Israel at the same time in an effort to annihilate the Jewish people.

THE RESPONSE FROM ISRAEL

Prime Minister Benjamin Netanyahu learns from Israeli Intelligence sources in the days leading up to the attack on Israel that a significant attack is being planned against his nation. In June of 2015 the Israeli Defensive Forces (IDF) instituted a plan to evacuate civilians from prospective battle zones in the case of conflict to prevent civilians from being used as human shields in any prospective war.[28] Prime Minister Netanyahu issues the order to evacuate civilians from prospective war zones into safe areas set aside in the nation of Israel.

The nation of Israel is attacked on all sides by the combined forces of all nations that are their immediate neighbors (the Psalm 83 coalition of nations) led by ISIS. There are too many attacking armies and the military forces of Israel are greatly outnumbered. ISIS prepares to deploy the nuclear weapon that will ensure the destruction of Israel.

Backed into a corner and faced with the total annihilation of his country, the Prime Minister of the Jewish state has little choice but to unleash the "Samson Option," the nuclear arsenal of Israel. Within moments his country is going to be hit by a nuclear device, and his armies are suffering from the combined onslaught of missiles and ground forces from all of the Islamic countries surrounding them. The chances of victory are nearly impossible, and the total destruction of Israel is practically guaranteed. The unthinkable thing happens. Israel releases their nuclear weapons in a last-ditch effort to save their country. The Psalm 83 scenario takes place. In the morning, as the smoke and fog of war clears, the attacking armies are simply gone.

---

28   Tzvi Ben-Gedalyahu, "IDF Source: Israel to Evacuate 1 million Lebanese in War on Hezbollah," *The Jewish Press*, June 4, 2015, http://www.jewishpress.com/news/breaking-news/idf-source-israel-to-evacuate-1-million-lebanese-in-war-on-hezbollah/2015/06/04.

They sought to accomplish the complete destruction of the nation of Israel, and instead, the destruction that they intended for God's promised people was turned back upon their own heads.

CAN THIS REALLY HAPPEN?

Could the scenario proposed above actually take place—or is this a work of pure science fiction? Perhaps it would be best for you to decide. The Psalm 83 scenario was laid out in detail in the pages of the Bible almost three thousand years ago. Just one hundred years ago, nothing proposed in Psalm 83 could have taken place. There was no nation of Israel in the Promised Land—and yet a miracle took place and the way was cleared for the Jews to return to their homeland against a powerful Islamic Caliphate based in Turkey. There was no nation of Israel until 1948—and then another miracle took place and the fledgling nation of Jewish people prevailed against overwhelming odds and managed to secure once again a place to call home. The nation of Israel did not control their capital city of Jerusalem, and then in 1967 another miracle happened. The Jewish people were able to seize control of Jerusalem and other lands that had been promised to them in the Six Day War despite being outnumbered nearly ten to one on the battlefield.

Time after time and in instance after instance, the nation of Israel has prevailed when any hope of success seemed a mere illusion to the world. The Lord gave the people of Israel a land grant that still has not been fulfilled to this day. After the Psalm 83 war, where Israel is forced to defend itself against a coalition of nations determined to erase them from the face of the earth, Israel will finally control the area of land that God said belongs to them. When Israel controls a nation, all others are welcomed into it and treated fairly regardless of their beliefs or religious associations. When ISIS controls areas in the Levant, Jews, Christians and even dissenting Muslims are systematically slaughtered.

THE WORLD'S RESPONSE TO THE PSALM 83 WAR

What will be the world's response in the aftermath of the Psalm 83 War? Will the world acknowledge that the nation of Israel has a right to defend itself when faced with certain annihilation? Interestingly enough, the chapter of the Bible that describes the city of Damascus becoming a "ruinous heap" also describes the people's response to this event.

> Oh the raging of many nations, they rage like the raging sea! Oh, the uproar of the peoples—they roar like the roaring of great waters! Although the peoples roar like the roar of surging waters, when he rebukes them they flee far away. (Isaiah 17:12-13 NIV)

The world is going to be furious with the nation of Israel. They will be incensed by the actions taken and will universally condemn the Jewish people. The United Nations will most likely move to denounce the nation of Israel. The Jewish people can certainly expect a new round of anti-Semitism and will become the target of all kinds of discrimination. It will most likely become like the 1930s all over again. Jews living outside of Israel will be targeted and suffer all kinds of abuse at the hands of their countrymen, often with the blessings of government officials. Being

Jewish could become one of the most dangerous things to acknowledge in the world. The rights and security of the Jewish people not dwelling in the Holy Land will vanish almost overnight. There will be new cries for a holocaust against the Jews, and many nations with Islamic ties will move to implement that strategy.

One thing will become apparent very quickly—the Jews will have to band together to survive. The land they will control after this war is far larger than the tiny nation they inhabit today. The new borders will stretch from the Nile River to the River Euphrates. The call will go out for the Jews to return home to the Promised Land, and many will heed that call because of the increased persecution in other countries. Many in the house of Israel will come home from the nations where they have been scattered for numerous centuries.

As the house of Israel regathers to their homeland, the United Nations will be seething from the audacity of Israel defending itself. The pressure on the United Nations to do something about what Israel has done will build until the UN is forced to act. Given the track record of resolutions that have not been favorable toward Israel, it's not hard to guess what the United Nations is going to do. There will be universal condemnation of Israel for the use of nuclear weapons, and the UN will pass a resolution saying that Israel can never use nuclear weapons again.

In order to appear fair, the United Nations will have to draft a resolution outlining when the use of force is justified, and which use of force can be employed in response to a given situation. There have never been any complete guidelines drafted by the UN that govern a "justifiable" use of force. The UN will be compelled to draft justifiable force guidelines that dictate an appropriate response when wars like the one that just occurred in the Middle East happen. But who can they turn to for guidance in drafting this politically sensitive document? Who can speak on this subject and carry the theological clout necessary to get the world to listen?

As the United Nations ponders this question, the Pope steps forward to offer his help on this sensitive matter. When the Pope offers his guidance and perspectives on the doctrine of a just war, he has just set the stage for the fulfillment of both Muslim and Catholic prophecies that paint a dark picture of what the future will be. It's time to examine those prophecies now.

CHAPTER NINE
PAPAL INTERVENTION AND CATHOLIC
END–TIME PROPHECIES

When Pope Francis steps forward to offer his insights on a just war, he is able to tap into a rich history of Catechisms (a handbook of questions and answers for teaching the principles of a religion) that have been codified by the Catholic Church. Many of these Catechisms have been handed down through the centuries, but have been modified in recent times to reflect the changing nature of our world. For example, the Catechisms governing warfare have been updated to reflect the changing nature of the weapons being used. Highly advanced weapons have capabilities to inflict destruction on a scale that was previously unknown and fall into their own category of consideration.

At the conclusion of the Psalm 83 war, the world will be looking for answers. When the Pope steps up to offer those answers, he will have the attention of the United Nations and the world like no other time. Here is one of the principles present in the "Just War Catechism" that the Pope may use when speaking to the world:

> Every act of war directed to the indiscriminate destruction of whole cities or vast areas with their inhabitants is a crime against God and man, which merits firm and unequivocal condemnation. A danger of modern warfare is that it provides the opportunity to those who possess modern scientific weapons—especially atomic, biological, or chemical weapons—to commit such crimes. (CCC2314)[29] [CCC means Catechism of the Catholic Church]

If the Pope cites this section of the Just War Doctrine, then to the uninformed it will appear as if the nation of Israel has committed a crime that merits condemnation. After all, the city of Damascus is going to be a "ruinous heap" and various sections in the countries of Lebanon, Jordan, Syria and Egypt are going to be "laid waste." The greater wrong against the nation of Israel, where the entire country was threatened with annihilation, will be largely ignored. Without complete understanding, and by downplaying the reality of the threat against Israel, it will be easy for the world to jump to conclusions and universally condemn the Jewish nation.

So we may gain complete understanding of the "Just War Doctrine," let's examine the exact words of this document.

---

29   Catholic Church Documents, "Just War Doctrine," Catholic Answers, http://www.catholic.com/documents/just-war-doctrine.

THE JUST WAR DOCTRINE

"The strict conditions for legitimate defense by military force require rigorous consideration. The gravity of such a decision makes it subject to rigorous conditions of moral legitimacy. At one and the same time:

► The damage inflicted by the aggressor on the nation or community of nations must be lasting, grave, and certain.

► All other means of putting an end to it must have been shown to be impractical or ineffective.

► There must be serious prospects of success.

► The use of arms must not produce evils and disorders graver than the evil to be eliminated. The power of modern means of destruction weighs very heavily in evaluating this condition.

► These are the traditional elements enumerated in what is called the "just war" doctrine. The evaluation of these conditions for moral legitimacy belongs to the prudential judgment of those who have responsibility for the common good." (CCC2309)

One of the tenets of this doctrine that justifies the use of force is that the potential damage to the country being attacked is "lasting, grave and certain." If those conditions are met, then it is not necessary that an aggressor nation strike first. A moral certainty is all that is needed to justify the defense of your nation. When a country is being attacked by overwhelming force using all munitions

available to the attackers, then you have certain justifi-
cation for defense. A country is even more justified when
threatened with nuclear weapons. With the certainty that
nuclear weapons are going to be used; then it is possible
for nations to use excessive destructive force when stop-
ping an aggressor.[30]

The Pope may not give all the pertinent facts and justifica-
tions the nation of Israel had when conducting the Psalm
83 war. If that happens, then it will be easy to condemn
the Jewish nation for their defensive actions against this
attack. The Scriptures say that the nations of the world are
going to "rage like roaring waters" when the details of this
war are made known. It doesn't sound like they are going
to be appeased and mollified by the words being spoken.
Instead the nations will be incensed and enraged in their
calls for punishment of Israel. In essence, the people of the
world may be trying to countermand and overrule what
God has set forth for the nation of Israel.

One thing should be noted here. Who is man to counter the
decree of God? Who is man to question what the Lord has
ordained and set apart for a land and a people? There is only
one area on the earth that the Lord has set aside for his
covenant people. It is a relatively small area in the huge ex-
panse of the earth. It's not even a particularly beautiful portion of our world, and yet man constantly sees fit to tell God
what He should be doing with this area. Oh the arrogance of
man to even presume to dictate to our Heavenly Father that
the land He has set apart for His people should be divided up
and given to others. Man does not decide what will happen
in the Lord's Promised Land, it is up to God.

---

30   Ibid.

Our Heavenly Father has constantly defended this area and cleared the way for His people to inhabit the land set aside for them. All that fight against Him will be defeated until the area for the nation of Israel is the exact size He declared when He set the boundaries for the house of Israel so long ago. Nothing that man can do will change that. All that have fought against the Lord in regard to His Promised Land have suffered the consequences and the group of nations coming against Israel in the Psalm 83 coalition will experience the same fate. The land for the house of Israel will be as the Lord decreed it. It's time for man to deal with that fact.

AFTER THE POPE SPEAKS

Some of the things the Pope has been saying lately have been highly controversial. For example, on May 13th of 2015 Pope Francis said that there should be a Palestinian State inside the current borders of Israel. These comments are in direct conflict with what the Lord has decreed for the Jewish state. This places the Pope on uncertain theological footing when he actively goes against what the Lord has decreed for this area. The Prime Minister of Israel immediately condemned these remarks shortly after they were made saying that the Pope's proposed actions would place the nation of Israel in jeopardy.

Not even one month later after making those comments, the Pope came out with his encyclical on climate change. On June 12th, 2015 it was reported by John Schnellhuber, one of the academics chosen by the Vatican to explain the Pope's recently released encyclical, that Pope Francis has "previously said the planet is overpopulated by at least six billion people."[31] This is a rather bold statement from someone who has lectured on the sanctity of human life. It could easily be construed by this statement that the Pope is promoting the genocide of six billion people currently living on the planet. Perhaps we should give the Pope the benefit of the doubt and conclude that his words were mis-construed or taken out of context. There is probably an explanation for his comments that was not reported.

In regard to the just war doctrine, at the conclusion of the Psalm 83 war, the world will be looking for guidance on how to deal with conflict. The Pope may insist that "Just War Guidelines" must be adhered to in the future, and that a force should be created to deal with future conflicts. In fact, it is certainly within the realm of possibility to think that the United Nations will set up an armed force to implement the guidelines proposed by the Pope. These armed forces will be following the directives that came down from Pope Francis in Rome, and thusly can be appropriately called the Roman Forces. They will be following the Pope's directives for the application of a just war. In this way, an armed force operating under the leadership of the Pope from Rome can easily be created. It would be entirely appropriate to call these soldiers the "Roman" army. The stage is now set for the fulfillment of several different prophecies—both Catholic and Muslim. Let's deal with the Catholic prophecies first.

THE PROPHECY OF THE POPES

The Catholic Church has some prophecies given by people well acknowledged by their church that have some rather disturbing things to say about end-time events and the

31   Alan Keyes, "Pope's Climate Agenda Could Bring Genocide," *World News Daily*, June 2015, http://www.wnd.com/2015/06/popes-climate-agenda-could-bring-genocide/.

fate of the Catholic Church. When relating these stories, it should be pointed out that when these prophecies are presented, it is in no way a criticism of the Catholic Church. They are presented with the hope that all can understand the prophecies presented, and then gain insight on how they relate to the events being described in the end-time narrative. With that understanding, let's examine the Prophecy of the Popes.

The Prophecy of the Popes was given by a man who foresaw the final pope. His name was Malachy O'Morgair or St. Malachy and he was born in Northern Ireland in the year 1094. He became the leader of the Catholic Church in Ireland and in 1139 went to Rome to seek an audience with the pope. He was brought in and met with Pope Innocent II, but came away from this encounter totally disillusioned for the future of the church. It was shortly after this encounter that St Malachy experienced a vision that foretold each and every pope that would inherit the Papacy in Rome until the final pope. He wrote down a list of the popes and some of the characteristics they would be known by until the final pope. He listed 112 popes, starting with the next pope, Pope Celestine II who began his reign in 1143, until the last pope, the 112th pope whom he characterized as Petrus Romanus.

What is alarming about this prophecy is not the accuracy with which St Malachy described the characteristics of each of these popes; but the fact that the final pope he listed in his prophecy, the 112th pope, was elected to the Papacy in 2013 and is now guiding the Catholic Church. The Prophecy of the Popes describes the final pope in the following manner:

> In extreme persecution, the seat of the Holy
> Roman Church will be occupied by Peter the
> Roman, who will feed the sheep through many
> tribulations; when they are over, the City of
> Seven Hills will be destroyed, and the terrible or
> fearsome Judge will judge his people.[32]

Did Malachy O'Morgair get it right? He called the 112th or
final pope "Petrus Romanus." Yet the 112th pope on his list
is the present pope of the Catholic Church and calls himself "Pope Francis" after his namesake "Francis of Assisi."
At first glance it would seem that this prophecy got it
wrong—until you dig deeper and look at the namesake the
current pope named himself after.

Francis of Assisi, the current pope's namesake, was born
Giovanni di Pietro di Bernardone on June 24th, 1182. The
last name "Pietro di Bernardone" literally means: **Peter
the Roman.**[33]

It is absolutely uncanny that a prophecy given over 900
years ago by St Malachy of the Catholic Church would nail
a prophecy so profoundly. The last name of Pope Francis's
namesake was literally **Peter the Roman.** The accuracy
with which he described the other popes leading up to the
current pope is uncanny also. I would highly recommend
the book "*Petrus Romanus*" by Thomas Horne and Chris
Putnam if you are curious about the other prophecies concerning the other popes.

The content of the prophecy of the final pope is highly
disturbing. It says that the Catholic Church is going to go

32 Thomas Horn and Chris Putnam, *Petrus Romanus*, (Crane, MO: Defender, 2012) p. 62.
33 Wikipedia, "Francis of Assisi," https://en.wikipedia.org/wiki/Francis_of_Assisi.

through "extreme persecution" and that "Peter the Roman will feed the sheep through many tribulations." It also says that the "City of Seven Hills," a common expression for the city of Rome, "will be destroyed." Considering the fact that Pope Francis has been described as the final pope in this prophecy, and is currently presiding over the Catholic Church, then this prophecy seems to gain more prominence when it coincides with the 70th Jubilee cycle where things will soon be changing in a profound manner. Certainly it is a time to be vigilant.

This Prophecy of the Popes is not the only prophecy that foretells a dreary future for the Catholic Church, the man leading the Catholic Church and the city of Rome. From the Catholic Church's own archives comes another prophecy that is similar to the Prophecy of the Popes. It is called the "Third secret of Fatima."

THE THIRD SECRET OF FATIMA

To find out more about this, we need to go back in time to that pivotal year in history, 1917. Remember, this was the year in history where the Balfour declaration was made paving the way for the reinstatement of the Jewish homeland and the year General Allenby captured Jerusalem and ousted the Ottoman Empire. Something else happened that year and this event profoundly affected the Catholic Church.

In Fatima, Portugal, on July 13th, 1917, three young Portuguese shepherds, Lucia Santos and her cousins Jacinta and Francisco Marto, received a series of apocalyptic visions and prophecies known as the "Three secrets of Fatima." It is the third secret that we are particularly interested in. When the third secret was finally revealed, it sent shock waves through the Catholic Church. The text of the third secret was officially released by the office of the Vatican on June 26th, 2000. Here is the official text of the Third Secret of Fatima:

I write in obedience to you, my God, who command me to do so through his Excellency the Bishop of Leiria and through your Most Holy Mother and mine. After the two parts which I have already explained, at the left of Our Lady and a little above, we saw an Angel with a flaming sword in his left hand; flashing, it gave out flames that looked as though they would set the world on fire; but they died out in contact with the splendor that Our Lady radiated towards him from her right hand; pointing to the earth with his right hand, the Angel cried out in a loud voice 'Penance, Penance, Penance!' And we saw in an immense light that is God; something similar to how people appear in a mirror when they pass in front of it, a Bishop dressed in White, we had the impression that it was the Holy Father. Other Bishops, Priests, men and women Religious going up a steep mountain, at the top of which there was a big Cross of rough-hewn trunks as of a cork-tree with the bark, before reaching there the Holy Father passed through a big city half in ruins and half trembling with halting step, afflicted with pain and sorrow, he prayed for the souls of the corpses he met on his way, having reached the top of the mountain, on his knees at the foot of the big Cross he was killed by a group of soldiers who fired bullets and arrows at him, and in the same way there died one after another the other Bishops, Priests, men and women

Religious, and various lay people of different ranks and positions. Beneath the two arms of the Cross there were two Angels each with a crystal aspersorium in his hand, in which they gathered up the blood of the Martyrs and with it sprinkled the souls that were making their way to God.[34]

Again, this is another text that seems to portray a bleak future for the city of Rome and the Vatican. Notice some of the descriptive elements of the story: a "big city half in ruins" and dead people lying in the streets as the pope passes them. The pope walks to the top of a steep mountain where "he was killed by a group of soldiers who fired bullets and arrows at him." Other religious leaders were killed at the same time as the pope. From what was described in the Third Secret of Fatima, we can certainly conclude that it involves the death of the pope by an army that has ransacked the city of Rome and carried out great destruction to "Roman" forces. In fact, this portrayal sounds like total victory over Roman forces by an army bent on their destruction.

There is an army out there who has promised to accomplish the exact thing that is spoken of in these two prophecies of the Catholic Church. It is an army led by the Caliphate and composed of Muslim forces. They have promised to march on Rome and to destroy the Vatican. They have even posted a picture of what this victory would look like. Here is an image of that picture:

---

34   Wikipedia, "Three Secrets of Fatima," http://en.wikipedia.org/wiki/Three_Secrets_of_F%c3%Altima.

Islamic State Flag being displayed over the Vatican

While most people do not believe something like this could ever happen, there are definitely prophecies contained in the archives of the Catholic Church that suggest the destruction of the city of Rome and the end of the papacy as we know it today. The Prophecy of the Popes predicts that Pope Francis will be the final pope in the Catholic Church, and the Third Secret of Fatima suggests that the pope will be killed by an army that ransacks the city of Rome. By the way, Fatima was the name of the daughter of Muhammad and it is very curious that this secret was given in a city that bears that identical name—Fatima, Portugal. The followers of an Islamic State led by the Caliphate have said time and time again they will march on Rome and destroy the Vatican. But how are they going to accomplish this feat?

The last time we were discussing an Islamic State we described how ISIS and the Caliphate of Abu Bakr al-Baghdadi were destroyed by Israel in the Psalm 83 war. If they were destroyed, then who is leading the charge to destroy the Vatican?

In the beginning of this book we discussed a power base that was controlling the Islamic religion, and how God's Word had diligently detailed the fate of those that would try to control this power. Just because ISIS has been destroyed does not mean that the power base was destroyed too. The power base is the office of the Caliphate. Once it has been reestablished, the power it represents will never be relinquished voluntarily. It represents too much authority and too much control over the Islamic people. The Caliphate represents the power to control over one billion people that profess to believe in Islam. The concentration of so much power in a single office is too tempting to ever let go of again. The right to control this power will be fought over and sought after by any who want to lead the body of Muslim believers.

Waiting patiently on the sidelines for Abu Bakr al-Baghdadi to make a fatal mistake was the nation of Turkey. What happens next will take the office of the Caliphate to heights that were unimaginable when Abu Bakr al-Baghdadi controlled it.

Before we describe those events, perhaps we should summarize the events leading up to the rise and fall of ISIS. It will help clarify the events that will happen after the Caliphate of Abu Bakr al-Baghdadi is no more.

CHAPTER TEN
THE EVENTS LEADING TO THE RISE AND FALL OF ISIS

Things can get confusing unless we stop to summarize what we have described so far. It has been a path where different prophecies seem to be foretelling divergent pathways and different outcomes, and yet now these prophecies are converging together in a remarkable fashion to tell a very similar story. Different worlds are colliding and yet the pictures presented in all end-time stories are becoming remarkably similar. Let's review some of the most notable facts.

- ▶ Al Qaeda (Iraq) emerged from the aftermath of the United States intervention in the nation of Iraq.

- ▶ A new leader arrived on the scene in Iraq and assumed absolute power over all Al Qaeda forces in Iraq on May 16th, 2010.

▶ His name is Abu Bakr al-Baghdadi and he consolidated his power by declaring a new "Islamic State of Iraq and the Levant" (ISIL) on April 8th, 2013. This group is also known as ISIS (Islamic State of Iraq and Syria) because of the area they control in Iraq and Syria.

▶ To assume absolute control over all Muslim believers, and to assist him in his quest to control the entire area of the Levant, Abu Bakr al-Baghdadi reestablished the office of the Caliphate on June 29th, 2014. The resurrection of the power base that controls all of Islam is just the thing that Abu Bakr thinks will lend him authority and get other Muslim nations to follow his commands.

▶ Abu Bakr and his minions in ISIS began a systematic terror campaign throughout the world to try to get the world to submit to ISIS. Over 1000 people that are non-combatants have been killed in attacks carried out in many nations. The attacks are ongoing to this day.

▶ The Caliphate of Abu Bakr created a humanitarian crisis when they began the systematic slaughter of any that will not follow the directives of the new caliph. Millions begin to flee the affected areas in Iraq and Syria starting in 2014, with the majority fleeing in 2015.

▶ ISIS troops have specifically targeted Christian groups living in the areas they control. Millions of Christians are displaced from these areas and those that cannot escape are killed and turned into sexual slaves for ISIS troops.

▶ ISIS has begun the slaughter of those they call infidels in Dabiq in order to provoke the armies of the world to come to Dabiq to fight an Islamic version of Armageddon. Abu Bakr believes in his vision of the battle in Dabiq so much that he commits countless atrocities to force this battle to come to pass.

▶ The Caliphate of Abu Bakr wants to control the entire area of the Levant. This includes the nation of Israel. Abu Bakr's desires place him in direct opposition to what the Lord has declared for the area of the Levant. The Lord has said the area from the river in Egypt (Nile) to the River Euphrates belongs to the nation of Israel. (Genesis 15:18)

▶ ISIS is able to get their hands on a nuclear weapon or weapons—possibly by manipulation from the nation of Iran and the proceeds from the Iranian Nuclear Deal. They intend to cause chaos in the world and move to use these weapons. Whether they are able to use these weapons on a nation outside of the Levant is unclear. ISIS has stated they will use nuclear weapons on other nations including the United States if they are able to get them. The United States government thought this threat credible enough that they conducted the Jade Helm nuclear response exercises in July to September of 2015 in order to prepare for just such a scenario.

- ► ISIS makes clear plans to control all the area of the Levant and plans a nuclear strike against any that oppose them. It is possible that Abu Bakr will use any nukes he has to strike other Muslim nations, or areas of resistance to his leadership. A prime example of this is the city of Damascus which is controlled by Bashar Assad and his Russian allies. A nuclear strike against Damascus by the Caliphate of Abu Bakr is certainly within the realm of possibility since those in that city are actively fighting against him.

- ► The Caliphate of Abu Bakr al-Baghdadi plans to consolidate his control over the entire Levant and the nation of Israel stands in his way. Abu Bakr plans a nuclear strike against Israel and the Israeli Defensive Forces learn of his plans and prepare to stop him. They prepare the Samson Option (a nuclear response when Israel is threatened with total annihilation). The use of the Samson Option will effectively turn the destruction intended for the Jewish people back upon the heads of their attackers. The nation of Israel moves to clear as many civilians from the potentially impacted areas as possible.

- ► Abu Bakr al-Baghdadi through the office of the Caliphate declares a "Holy War" (Jihad) against Israel and calls on all Islamic nations in the Levant to attack the Jewish people and follow the lead of ISIS. The nations of Lebanon, Jordan, Egypt and the Palestinians heed the call and begin attacking the nation of Israel with ISIS leading the way. They have overwhelming numerical superiority and begin to gain ground on all fronts.

▶ The coalition of nations coming against Israel was described in the Bible in Psalm 83. The Jewish people have little choice but to respond in kind to the force being used against them. There are places in the Bible that suggest a radiation-like sickness affecting the land and the people of Northern Israel with lean harvests and the people suffering from disease and incurable pain. (Isaiah 17:4-6, 10-11) This could certainly be the description of a nuclear event striking limited areas in Israel. If any type of nuclear device or a dirty bomb (a bomb designed to spread radioactive nuclear waste to contaminate an area) were ever used against Israel then there is no doubt what Israel's response would be. They would unleash their nuclear weapons to counter and neutralize any threat against their nation.

▶ The description of what happens to the nations coming against Israel presented in the Bible certainly sounds like what you would expect if nuclear weapons were involved. The only other way to achieve the results of what happens to these attacking nations would be to have a world-wide catastrophic event. A nuclear response from Israel is the most logical explanation of vast areas of land being laid waste. Some of the most modern nuclear weapons have destructive potential that does not irradiate the area for long periods of time where they are used. Thus the land would be inhabitable shortly after the use of nuclear weapons.

▶ Whatever decimates the attacking coalition of nations coming against Israel happens over the duration of one night. It begins in the evening, and by the morning the event is accomplished. (Isaiah 17:13-14)

▶ At the conclusion of this war, the area set aside for the nation of Israel by the Lord will become available to them. The house of Israel will gain access to their ancestral homeland and will have new borders with new neighbors and all of the problems that will bring.

▶ ISIS and the Caliphate of Abu Bakr al-Baghdadi will be destroyed at the conclusion of the Psalm 83 war. The destruction they intended for the nation of Israel will be returned upon their own heads. The Levant will be controlled by the house of Israel in fulfillment of the prophecy given in Genesis 15:18.

Many may consider the events portrayed above to be too strong of a statement for the fate of ISIS. After all, many of the things described above have not even happened. Yet these events are clearly portrayed in the pages of the Bible. Whether you choose to believe them or not is up to you. ISIS and the Caliphate of Abu Bakr al-Baghdadi are going to be destroyed. Even without the prophetic input from the Bible, there are historic precedents that suggest that ISIS will be destroyed because of some of the things they have done.

Let's discuss one of the most profound historical prece-dents that suggest that ISIS is going to suffer a humiliating fate. It involves a period in history where another Muslim coalition under the direction of a Caliphate committed some heinous crimes against humanity. The time I am referring to involved Muslim forces during the rule of the Ottoman Empire. Please notice the time frame involved also.

In the year 1915, the office of the Caliphate, in conjunction with the government of the Ottoman Empire, ordered the extermination of Armenian Christians living within the borders of the Empire. Working hand in hand, Muslim troops under directions from the Caliphate, worked with Turkish government troops to accomplish the genocide of the Armenian Christians. As previously described, the Armenian Christians were marched into the mountains where they were killed, or were led into the desert on endless walks without food or water until they died. Official estimates place the number of Armenian Christians killed at one and a half million people.

If you fast forward 100 years, we find that another Caliphate, the Caliphate of Abu Bakr al-Baghdadi, has ordered almost the identical crime in an area close to the original genocide. Abu Bakr ordered the slaughter and enslavement of Yezidi Christians, Syrian Christians, Iraqi Christians and more Armenian Christians. The vast majority of these crimes took place in the year 2015, exactly 100 years from the time it previously occurred. The Ottomans began the extermination of the Armenian Christians on April 24th, 1915. History seems to be repeating itself in 100 year intervals. Is this the only event that happened in a 100 year interval? Previously we mentioned the reestablishment of the Caliphate on June 29th, 2014—and 100 years previously almost to the very day, June 28th, 1914, an assassination took place that set in motion the First World War. Germany emerged as the primary aggressor in both of the World

Wars. The office of the Caliphate will be the power behind the aggression in the Islamic world that sets the world on fire in future armed conflicts.

What happened to the Ottoman Empire after it engaged in the wholesale slaughter of 1.5 million Armenian Christians? The empire that had been a player on the world scene for 600 years ceased being an empire within three years after committing this act of genocide. Furthermore, the office of the Caliphate was abolished on March 3rd, 1924—a scant nine years from the perpetration of this crime against humanity. The office of the Caliphate was instituted after the death of Muhammad in 632 and had lasted almost 1300 years. It wasn't until the Caliphate cooperated in the death of so many Christians that it was destroyed the first time.

Will the renewed office of the Caliphate established by Abu Bakr al-Baghdadi on June 29th, 2014, be any different from the first after they have orchestrated the wholesale slaughter of Christians living in the Middle East?

There were two historical precedents set by the acts of the Ottoman Empire:

1. Any aggressors or empire that engages in the wholesale annihilation of Christians or Jews or other people will be militarily defeated after the act has been committed. Another example of this is what happened to the Nazis in WWII after they initiated the Holocaust of the Jews.

2. If those atrocities were committed at the behest of a religious office, such as the Caliphate, then that religious office will eventually be destroyed or rendered inoperable.

If what has happened in the past is any guide, then the office of the Caliphate is on a time clock counting down to the time it will be destroyed. Abu Bakr al-Baghdadi was the first to control the renewed office of the Caliphate, but he will not be the last to attempt to control it. Others will attempt to seize the power of the Caliphate, and the Bible has described what will happen to them also.

Historical precedent would argue that Abu Bakr has but a short time left before the events of the Psalm 83 war overwhelm him. The office of the Caliphate was not abolished with the defeat of the Ottoman Empire. It continued on for seven years (until 1924) after Turkish forces fled the city of Jerusalem (1917) as they were defeated by the armed forces of General Allenby. When ISIS and Abu Bakr al-Baghdadi are killed during the Psalm 83 war, the office of the Caliphate will continue on. It will be seized by another Muslim leader even hungrier for power than Abu Bakr.

It is the premise of this book that restoring the Caliphate, the power base behind the Muslim quest for world domination, will set events in motion that will eventually lead to World War III. What we are currently seeing is a proxy war being fought with the major players on the sidelines not fully engaged in this war. When the Psalm 83 war takes place, a whole series of cataclysmic events will occur that set in motion end-time events written about in the Bible.

The death of Abu Bakr al-Baghdadi and his ISIS soldiers will not lead to the end of the Caliphate system immediately. The office of the Caliphate and the power it represents will be shifted to another country. This new country will pick up where Abu Bakr left off. Let's discuss how this might happen.

CHAPTER ELEVEN
THE AFTERMATH OF THE DEFEAT OF ISIS

In the aftermath of the Psalm 83 war, ISIS has been defeated and Abu Bakr al-Baghdadi has been killed. His hopes to lead the Muslim world through the office of the Caliphate have been shattered. If Abu Bakr is dead and ISIS is destroyed, then that means that the prophecy attributed to Muhammad concerning the battle of Dabiq has not yet been fulfilled. Remember, this prophecy claims that Muslim forces triumph over the forces of Rome in an Islamic version of Armageddon. This is one of the only predictive prophecies ever attributed to Muhammad. Let's assume that this prophecy is true. If this is the case, then how did Abu Bakr get this prophecy wrong?

Perhaps we should look at the prophecy of Dabiq again and see where Abu Bakr erred. Let's pay careful attention to the exact words of the prophecy:

> The Last Hour would not come until the Romans would land at al-Amaq or in Dabiq. An army

consisting of the best (soldiers) of the people of the earth at that time will come from Medina (to counteract them)...They will then fight and a third of the army would run away, whom Allah will never forgive. A third which would be constituted of excellent martyrs in Allah's eye would be killed and the third who would never be put to trial would win and they would be conquerors of Constantinople. (Muhammad, according to Hadith)

One of the most glaring errors Abu Bakr made was to ignore where a portion of the army of Dabiq comes from. It says they come from "Medina." Medina is one of the holy sites of the Muslim religion and is located in Saudi Arabia. Abu Bakr never had any support from the nation of Saudi Arabia—in fact the Saudis were actively opposed to him and constantly fought against him. The army of ISIS was never composed of any significant number of Saudis. This was his first mistake.

We are given another clue concerning the errors of Abu Bakr when it says that parts of the army of Dabiq would be the "conquerors of Constantinople." Who are the conquerors of Constantinople? The conquerors of Constantinople are still there—they are the Islamic Turkish forces that conquered that city and then renamed it "Istanbul." They have been in control of this city for hundreds of years and they are definitely Muslim forces from the nation of Turkey. Abu Bakr never had any significant support from the nation of Turkey—so again we see another glaring error made by the deceased leader of the Caliphate. He was constantly at war with the nation of Turkey and his ISIS forces carried out terrorist attacks in various cities in Turkey.

While Abu Bakr may have been mistaken, we get an important clue to the identity of the nation that may be controlling the troops in the Dabiq prophecy by the name of the city given. Constantinople was the name given to this city by the Romans. When Muslim forces seized control of this city after the defeat of the Eastern leg of the Roman Empire, they renamed it Istanbul. They were distinctly Turkish Muslim forces—so the real leader of the Muslim forces in the Dabiq prophecy must come from the nation of Turkey. This makes perfect sense since the nation of Turkey wants the prestige associated with leading the Muslim World. In the eyes of the Turks, the best way to achieve this goal is to return the office of the Caliphate to the nation of Turkey—a nation that controlled the Caliphate for over 500 years.

There is absolutely no doubt that Turkey will seize the office of the Caliphate after Abu Bakr has been killed in the Psalm 83 war. The current president of Turkey, Recep Tayyip Erdogan, has wanted to be the leader of the Caliphate ever since it was reestablished in June of 2014. In August of 2014, Erdogan moved the nation of Turkey to a Presidential system, and assumed the office of the president on August 28th, 2014. His presidential system was designed to look exactly as it would if he were to control the Caliphate. Erdogan made his desire to control the Caliphate official recently and is taking steps to make his dream a reality.

On December 27th, 2015, a spokesman for Erdogan named Hayrettin Karaman, said openly that Erdogan would soon become the caliph for all Muslims. In Yen Safak, the official state newspaper for Turkey, Karaman wrote the following:

> During the debate on the presidential system here is what everyone must do while taking into

account the direction of the world's national interest and the future of the country and not focus on the party or a particular person. What this [presidential system] looks like is the **Islamic Caliphate system** in terms of its mechanism. In this system the people choose the leader, the **Prince**, and then all will pledge the Bay'ah [allegiance] and then the chosen president appoints the high government bureaucracy and he cannot interfere in the judiciary where the Committee will audit legislation independent of the president. (Hayrettin Karaman)[35]

Erdogan is setting himself up to be the new caliph and wants to assume control of the office of the Caliphate. There is no other leader in the Muslim world saying they will soon control the Caliphate like President Erdogan is saying. He fully intends to seize control of this office, and everything he does is geared toward that goal. Even the state newspapers in Turkey are printing these statements. People in Turkey consider the loss of the Caliphate in 1924 a deep wound that needs to be healed. There are billboards posted all around Istanbul that say "Yeniden Dirilis, Yeniden Yukselis," which means "Resurrection Again, Rising Again."[36] This statement is in direct reference to the loss of the Caliphate and the power of the Ottoman Empire, a power and an empire the Turks want to establish again. Make no mistake, the Muslim believers in Turkey want the Caliphate and the glory of the Ottoman Empire to return again, and President Erdogan is just the man to make this happen.

35 Walid Shoebat, "Erdogan Has Just Been Declared The Leader Of The Entire Muslim World, Muslims Are Already Calling Him God," Shoebat.com, December 27, 2015, http://shoebat.com/2015/12/27/90032/.
36 Ibid.

To prepare the way for the return of the Caliphate system to Turkey, President Erdogan has built a huge presidential palace, consisting of more than 1005 rooms in Bestepe, Turkey. He plans to have representatives from all Islam Union nations meet with him in his presidential palace. In this way, all Muslim nations can participate in advising the new caliph and feel that they have some input in the direction the Caliphate system is taking.

Everything is prepared and President Erdogan is waiting for the time when he can finally control the office of the Caliphate. The death of Abu Bakr al-Baghdadi and the destruction of ISIS is the lynch pin that will set these events into motion. This crucial event will also set into motion other key events on the Lord's prophetic time clock. Let's summarize these events and other points in the critical time frame around the conclusion of the Psalm 83 war.

AFTER THE CONCLUSION OF THE PSALM 83 WAR

▶ ISIS and the attacking nations of the Psalm 83 coalition of nations will be defeated.

▶ Israel will have new borders that expand up to Turkey in the north, Iraq and Iran to the east, Saudi Arabia to the south, and Egypt and the Sudan to the west.

- ▶ The world will condemn Israel for the defensive actions they took and the use of the Samson Option which preserved their nation with the use of nuclear weapons.

- ▶ The United Nations will meet to propose legislation to prevent Israel from ever using nuclear weapons again. A controversy will arise since the groundwork legislation for the proper components of a "just war" have never been officially established by the United Nations. The UN will search for answers on how a "just war" can be conducted.

- ▶ Pope Francis will step forward to offer his thoughts on a just war. He will use guidelines from the catechisms of the Catholic Church to propose just war rules for future conflicts. Some of the things he says may inflame hatred toward the nation of Israel and the Vatican, especially among the Muslim nations. Many Islamic countries will feel that Israel did not follow proper guidelines when conducting the Psalm 83 war.

- ▶ The "Just War" guidelines offered by the pope will infuriate many Muslim nations and make the pope and the Vatican a target for Islamic aggression. The promise of the slain leader of the Caliphate (Abu Bakr al-Baghdadi) to march on Rome and conquer Rome will no longer be an idle threat. Muslim forces sacked Rome and the Vatican in 856, and the quest to accomplish this goal once again will become foremost on the minds of many Muslims.

► Many of the peacekeepers in the United Nations trying to enforce the "Just War Doctrine" will become known as "Roman" forces since they are following the dictates of the Pontiff of Rome. Also the threat of Islamic aggression against Italy may cause the Italian or "Roman" army to be strengthened to meet the new threat. A "Roman" army is now in existence to fulfill the prophecy of Dabiq.

► President Recep Tayyip Erdogan of Turkey steps forward to seize the office of the Caliphate upon the death of Abu Bakr. The office of the Caliphate is moved back to the nation of Turkey that controlled it previously for 500 years. President Erdogan assumes the role of the new caliph directing the Caliphate and invites other Muslim countries to send representatives to Turkey so they can have a say in the direction of the new Caliphate. President Erdogan has plans to make the Caliphate the most powerful institution on the face of the earth. The world will tremble when Erdogan speaks as the mouthpiece of all of Islam—because he now has 1.5 billion followers listening to everything he says, ready to carry out his every command. The former power of the Ottoman Empire will be surging again, ready to retake its prominence in world history.

► The fall of the murderous regime of ISIS should bring a time of relative tranquility to the Earth. Instead of a time of peace, one of the worst times to ever face mankind is just about to begin.

Stepping to the forefront of world history is a man that the Bible describes as the "Chief Prince" of a power base located in the nation of Turkey. Onto the world stage steps the man who will be "**GOG.**"

CHAPTER TWELVE
THE RISE OF GOG AND THE NATION OF TURKEY

Just who is Gog and where does he come from? We have another mystery we need to decipher. The reference to Gog comes from the Bible from the book of Ezekiel. Let's take a look at that passage so we can gain some insight into what God's Word is referring to.

> The word of the Lord came to me: Son of man, set your face against Gog, of the land of Magog, the chief prince of Meshech and Tubal... (Ezekiel 38:1-2 NIV)

Gog is apparently a leader of some kind that brings a coalition of nations against Israel after they have been established in their land again in modern times. There are few precedents given in the Bible for the leader given the title "Gog." The closest identification is the ancient king Gyges, the king of Lydia in 660 BC. Lydia is the ancient name given for the land of Turkey. The name seems to be intentionally vague and stands for an enemy of God's people.

The land of Magog is a geographical location and a name-sake. Magog was one of the sons of Japheth, a son of Noah, and denotes the name of a people and where they came to reside. The ancestors of Magog settled in the area of central Turkey, so Magog is clearly associated with the modern day nation of Turkey.

Two other enigmatic places mentioned in this passage are associated with the modern day nation of Turkey also. Meshech and Tubal were sons of Japheth also and their ancestors ended up residing north of Israel in Turkey in Asia Minor. The *Moody Atlas of Bible Lands* can be of great assistance to us when trying to locate a geographical land area where these people came to reside.

As you can see, Magog, Meshech and Tubal are all firmly located in the nation of Turkey. The closest namesake for Gog, Gyges, king of Lydia, was a ruler in the land of Turkey in ancient times. It's as if the Bible is trying to highlight the nation of Turkey as the center of a power base that comes against Israel in a climatic end-times battle. Let's look at the entire passage in Ezekiel that lists the nations coming against Israel in this upcoming war.

Son of man, set your face against Gog, of the land of Magog, the chief prince of Meshech and Tubal; prophesy against him and say: 'This is what the Sovereign Lord says: I am against you, O Gog, chief prince of Meshech and Tubal. I will turn you around, put hooks in your jaws and bring you out with your whole army—your horses, your horsemen fully armed, and a great horde with large and small shields, all of them brandishing their swords. Persia, Cush and Put will be with them, all with shields and helmets, also Gomer with all its troops, and Beth Togarmah from the far north with all its troops—the many nations with you. (Ezekiel 38:2-6 NIV)

This passage is describing a future war where different groups of people band together to attack Israel in modern times. When we look at the list of the people and nations that come together for this attack against Israel, we see two more groups that are identified with the nation of Turkey. Gomer and Togarmah are two more areas that are currently located in Turkey as you can see on the *Moody Atlas of Bible Lands*. That places five members of the attacking coalition in the nation of Turkey with Gog being the "chief prince" that leads this coalition. Turkey is being highlighted as the area to pay special attention to; and Gog is the leader that provides the impetus for the upcoming attack on Israel. The nation of Turkey is the power base that Gog relies upon—he is their chief prince and leader.

The *Moody Atlas of Bible Lands* is not the only source that places Meshech, Tubal, Magog, Gomer and Togarmah firmly in ancient Turkey. Some of the most prestigious Bible reference books, such as the *Macmillan Bible Atlas*, and the *Oxford Bible Atlas* also place these five entities in Turkey.

The other participants in this attack are more easily identified. "Persia, Cush, and Put will be with them, all with shields and helmets..." (Ezekiel 38:5)

Persia is the modern day nation of Iran—so it appears that Iran will be giving tentative help to this attacking coalition even though they have an ulterior motive in doing so. Iran wants the "Twelfth Imam" to come out of hiding to lead the entire Muslim world, but if they have any opportunity to destroy the "Little Satan," as they call Israel, they will take it. If an army led by the Caliphate could be destroyed at the same time—this may be the catastrophe Iran is looking for to force the Twelfth Imam out of hiding. Therefore, the nation of Iran will support this coalition.

Cush is the area immediately south of Egypt and is the area now called Sudan. Sudan became the "Islamic Republic of Sudan" in 1989 and has become a hotbed of Islamic repression against Christianity and other religions since then.

Put is identified as Libya and is the area west of Egypt in the modern day nation of Libya and includes small areas of Algeria and Tunisia also. Libya was the site of the attack on the US Diplomatic Compound in Benghazi by Islamic forces on September 11th, 2012.

One characteristic of all the areas and nations identified as aggressors in Ezekiel thirty eight is that they are all Islamic nations. Turkey, Iran, Sudan, Libya, Algeria and Tunisia are all Islamic nations. They are separate and diverse Islamic cultures, with some being Sunni Muslims and others Shia Muslims, but they are all Islamic nations.

So that we may more clearly identify the attacking coalition in the Gog/Magog war, let's list the people and the nations they are associated with in the upcoming war.

GOG/MAGOG COALITION:

- ▶ Gog: the leader of the Magog forces

- ▶ Magog: Turkey

- ▶ Meshech: Turkey

- ▶ Tubal: Turkey

- ▶ Gomer: Turkey

- ▶ Togarmah: Turkey

- ▶ Persia: Iran

- ▶ Cush: Sudan

- ▶ Put: Libya and parts of Algeria and Tunisia

Now we have some clues to the identity of Gog based on identifying factors in the Bible. He arises from a power base centered in Turkey and is the "chief prince" or leader of this power base. He has the power and authority to lead other Muslim nations in an attack against Israel. The nations participating in this attack are all Muslim nations. The Lord is against Gog and his attacking forces.

From this description in the Bible, can we draw any conclusions to whom Gog might be? Do we even have to draw our own conclusions when those describing a leader in Turkey right now are using the same descriptive elements the Bible uses to describe a man that wants to take over the office of the Caliphate and is the leader of Turkey today?

The spokesman for presidential authority in Turkey, Hyrettin Karaman, said the following on December 27th, 2015 about the presidential system in Turkey:

> What this [presidential system] looks like is the
> **Islamic Caliphate system** in terms of its mecha-
> nism. In this system the people chose the lead-
> er, the **Prince**, and then all will pledge Bay'ah
> [allegiance]...[37]

Mr. Karaman is using the same descriptive element the
Bible uses when describing the President of Turkey, Recep
Tayyip Erdogan. The Bible uses the term "chief prince"
when describing the leader of the Magog coalition of forces. People in Turkey are calling their president "the prince"
when talking about Erdogan. The descriptive title "chief
prince" means that this person is the supreme leader of
this coalition of nations. The people of Turkey use the title
"the prince" to describe their president whom they feel
should be leading the Caliphate.

**Could President Erdogan of Turkey be the mysterious lead-
er the Bible calls Gog?** If President Erdogan takes control
of the Caliphate upon the death of Abu Bakr, he will have
a powerful force supporting him and propelling him to
power. President Erdogan already controls the five powerful groups located in Turkey that make him the leader of
the Gog/Magog alliance. He controls the area of Magog,
Meshech, Tubal, Gomer and Togarmah—all located in the
nation of Turkey. He has already built the palace where representatives of all Muslim nations can gather to govern the
body of Muslim believers. He has set Turkey up as the me-
diator of all peace agreements in the Middle East—making
Turkey the power broker that can make or break all deals
made in the Middle East. Turkey is the link that Europe uses
for Middle Eastern negotiations. They were once going to

37 Walid Shoebat, "Erdogan Has Just Been Declared The Leader Of The Entire Muslim World, Muslims Are Already Calling Him God," Shoebat.com, December 27, 2015, http://shoebat.com/2015/12/27/90032/.

be a part of the European Union and Europe still uses those ties when dealing in the Middle East. In many ways, Turkey is the key to the future leadership in the Middle East.

President Erdogan knows all these facts and is exploiting his position of power to seize control of the Caliphate and make Turkey a force to be reckoned with in the future. If President Erdogan is not the man who will be Gog, then he is a very close prototype to what we can expect when Gog rises to power. One thing is very certain—Turkey will be a nation the world cannot ignore much longer. Gog will arise from the nation of Turkey to seize control of the Caliphate and unite the Muslim nations into the most powerful fighting force on the face of the earth with 1.5 billion Muslims following him.

Gog will not tolerate any rivals to his power. That means there are several problem areas that will have to be dealt with after he comes to power.

1. The pope presents a threat to his leadership. The Catholic Church has over one billion members and this threat to the Muslim quest for world dominion must be dealt with. Gog must destroy the Catholic Church and the way to do that is to destroy the office of the pope and not allow any more popes to be chosen by the Vatican. Gog will move to assassinate Pope Francis and then will occupy the Vatican and not allow the surviving Cardinals to elect another pope. The leadership of the Catholic Church will effectively end.

2. The European Union must be dealt with. Europe stood in the way and blocked the spread of Islam throughout the world before

in the middle ages. Gog will do everything in his power to make sure this does not happen again. The major European nations have been weakened by faltering economies and population decline. Huge numbers of Muslims have been allowed into these countries through out of control emigration policies and the refugee crisis. While the vast majority of these Muslims are law abiding citizens of their host countries, some of these Muslims have been actively working against these nations to destabilize the governments and establish Sharia law over the laws of the land where they reside. Many would not resist if the Caliphate were to mandate active aggression against Europe. If Gog were to declare jihad against any of the European countries, he would have a sizable force to contend with already living in each of these nations. All of Europe would be in serious trouble.

3. Gog knows the United States is the most powerful nation in the world militarily. But we are also a nation that is at war with itself politically. Instead of dealing with our issues in a straightforward and conciliatory manner, each political party blames the other for all of the issues that are facing us and the problems are getting larger. Personal responsibility is vacant on our national stage. We have allowed the debt facing our nation to rise to the point where it threatens our stability. We have become the biggest debtor nation in the history of the world. The leader known as Gog will exploit all of our weaknesses and attempt

to neutralize us on the world stage. The only hope for the United States is if we turn back to the Lord. We must work together to solve our problems—not against each other. The United States will be great again when the values taught by Jesus Christ are the guiding principles that direct our actions in the world. Until then, Gog and his Islamic Caliphate will do everything in his power to stop us.

4. The forces of Gog will have to deal with the nation of Israel. Israel has been a thorn in the side of Islam since 1917 when the way was cleared for them to return to the land set aside for them by the Lord. Gog is going to gather the largest army ever assembled and attack the nation of Israel with the intention of wiping Israel off the map. He will have over-whelming numerical superiority to the point that Gog will feel there is no way for him to lose. In the eyes of Gog, the time of his great-est victory will be when the nation of Israel is no more.

Power, greed, world dominion, an Islamic dynasty that controls the world and the death of any rivals—these are the things Gog wants and will do everything in his power to possess. Much more than that, Gog has the ability to bring war to the earth on a global scale. It's time to discuss the exploits of the man who will be Gog and the fate that awaits him on his path to world dominion.

CHAPTER THIRTEEN
THE EXPLOITS AND THE FATE OF GOG

Gog is going to assume control of the office of the Caliphate after Abu Bakr is defeated. He will then move to unite the Muslim world into a political union that can't be ignored. The first thing to be dealt with is a Muslim world reeling from defeat. Israel engineered a resounding victory in the Psalm 83 war and Gog must work to get the Islamic world back on track.

One of the best ways for Gog to do that is to point out the fact that Abu Bakr al-Baghdadi needed to be destroyed—he had waged war against other Muslims instead of uniting all of Islam. Gog will point out that if the Muslim nations were united, then they would be unstoppable against all that oppose them. He will then move to unite the Islamic world by bringing up a cause that all Muslims will agree with—the universal condemnation of Israel for their tactics in the recent war.

Gog will then call for a united council of all Muslim nations to be held in his home country of Turkey. He has a palace in Turkey at Bestepe ready for a meeting such as this.

The 1005 Room Presidential Palace in Bestepe, Turkey Set Up by President Erdogan

They will convene in the palace for the express purpose of dealing with the Jewish problem. When they are finished with this meeting, two things will have happened. Gog will emerge as the leader of the Muslim world with the office of the Caliphate bestowed upon him, and Muslim nations will universally call for sanctions and punishment against the nation of Israel for their use of nuclear weapons in the Psalm 83 war. Gog will then make a series of demands that the world must comply with or be threatened with war. As Gog rises to power, the world will become a far more perilous place to live.

No one knows for sure how things are going to happen, but the following scenario ties together the prophecies of Muslims and Catholics with those in the Bible to form a seamless way the differing prophecies may fit together and come to pass. Here's how the scenario may play out:

The Muslim nations will demand retaliation against the state of Israel, and if the United Nations does not comply immediately with those demands then Gog, in his role as the new leader of the Caliphate, will declare jihad against all who will not comply with his demands.

Many of the Muslims already embedded in the European nations will begin to carry out acts of war in their host nations when decisive action is not taken against Israel. England, France and Germany already have sizable populations of Muslims residing in their countries, as well as many other European nations. Even if only ten per cent of these Muslims carry out the will of the Caliphate, that is still a significant number of people. When you add 1.8 million illegal border crossings by bands of Middle Eastern refugees on the outer borders of the European Union in 2015—then Europe has a sizable problem to contend with.[38] Europe will reel as terrorist acts are carried out throughout their lands and governments try to restore order in the chaos.

Because of renewed anti-Semitism, Jewish people will begin returning to Israel from the various nations in the world where they have been dispersed. The persecution against the Jews will reach levels not seen since the days of WWII. The influxes of all those in the house of Israel will help fill the land within the new borders of the nation of Israel. Being a Jew outside Israel will almost be intolerable as the world acts to condemn the Jewish nation.

As violence escalates, the pope will step forward to offer his guidelines for a just war in an attempt to calm the anarchy reigning in the European nations. His attempts will result in United Nations troops being sent to particular hot spots in order to quell the uprisings and restore order. Muslims will regard the pope as an enemy because he will be seen as the leader uniting Roman forces against Islam.

---

38   Lorne Cook and Menelaos Hadjicostis, "EU, Turkey reach migrant deal," *Spokesman-Review*, 19 March 2016, p. 3.

One of the sites of particular unrest will be an area just outside the new northern border of Israel near the southern border of Turkey. Muslim troops will flock to this hotspot in an effort to provoke a new confrontation with the nation of Israel and any who will stand in their way. United Nations troops will flood this area in order to prevent all-out war from engulfing the Middle East once again. Tensions will rise until the situation rapidly escalates out of control. An all-out shooting war will erupt when anger explodes in this cauldron of emotions. The name of this place—is Dabiq.

To many Muslims, Dabiq will be the rallying point for the new found power of the Islamic religion. Islamic forces will rout the forces of the United Nations in Dabiq. The Muslim world will have their version of Armageddon and the victory that has so often eluded them.

The Islamic forces of Gog will have renewed confidence from their victory at Dabiq. They will move to forcibly spread Islam throughout the world.

Because of the actions of Gog—war will be unleashed on the whole world. Gog is characterized in the Bible as having a bow (a symbol of war) in his left hand. (Ezekiel 39:3) World War III will begin in earnest.

Islamic forces will invade Italy with the Vatican as their target. Rome will be attacked and Gog's forces will overwhelm the Vatican. The pope will be killed in these attacks leaving no rival to Gog's power. The pope's death will be the fulfillment of the Prophecy of the Popes, and the Third Secret of Fatima prophecies. Ironically, it will be Fatima's (the daughter of Muhammad) ancestors that fulfill this prophecy.

As Islamic forces are waging war across the world, Gog plans for the ultimate destruction of the nation of Israel. He amasses a huge army and plans a surprise attack on the people of Israel. This army will be so large that it will be practically impossible for the Jewish people and the house of Israel to fend off the attack. Gog has numerical superiority to the point that it won't matter what Israel does—he is virtually assured a victory when his massive army strikes the Jews.

With his gigantic army in position, Gog prepares to strike the nation of Israel. In Gog's mind, there is no way he can lose. Just as he is about to give the order to attack—something happens. It is so unexpected that Gog can't believe it is happening. As Gog watches this event unfold, a feeling of absolute terror overwhelms him. His meticulous plans begin to unravel right before his eyes.

What happens to Gog? How are his plans disrupted?

When Gog's plans interfere with what our Heavenly Father has decreed for the nation of Israel, then the Lord will move to overrule the plans of the Caliphate based in Turkey. This time there will be no question whether Israel is justified in defending themselves. The Lord will move to defend Israel and will intervene in the protection of His chosen people. Just how the Lord does this is the topic of the next chapter.

CHAPTER FOURTEEN
THE FATE OF GOG AND HIS HORDES

How can anyone know what will happen to Gog and the massive army he has arrayed against Israel? How can anyone presume to speculate about the fate of a mysterious character that has not even appeared in his role as Gog on the world stage?

No man can know these things—and yet the Bible contains the words meticulously detailing the fate of Gog and his gigantic army. And this description was written over 2500 years ago. The events that will soon be overtaking Gog and the world were written outside the dimension of time and were written for our instruction and understanding. We were not left without insight regarding these events since the Bible has described these things in detail for us. Whether we choose to seek out those answers is entirely up to us. The fate that awaits Gog was detailed on the pages of the Old Testament book of Ezekiel. Man may not be able to see the future but the Lord can. Let's take a look at what the Bible has to say about Gog.

Gog has amassed his forces and comes against the modern day nation of Israel with their new boundaries from the Psalm 83 War. Israel has been living in relative peace and safety in their land since the Psalm 83 War and is not expecting an all-out assault against them.

The prophet Ezekiel describes the rise of Gog and his massive army as they come to annihilate the land of Israel.

> After many days you will be called to arms. In future years you will invade a land that has recovered from war, whose people were gathered from many nations to the mountains of Israel, which had long been desolate. They had been brought out from the nations, and now all of them live in safety. (Ezekiel 38:8 NIV)

Notice how this verse says that Israel has "recovered from war." This is the Psalm 83 War where Israel defended its right to exist as a nation and gained the land that the Lord says belongs to them. Notice also how this verse says that Israel had regathered to the land "from the nations." The intense anti-Semitism after the Psalm 83 War will force many of the house of Israel back to the land that our Heavenly Father has prepared for them. Also this verse says, "now all of them live in safety." There will be relative peace in the land of Israel and the Jewish nation will not expect to be attacked.

Next, Ezekiel says what Gog will say when he comes to invade Israel. "You will say, 'I will invade a land of unwalled villages, I will attack a peaceful and unsuspecting people—all of them living without walls and without gates and bars.'" (Ezekiel 38:11 NIV)

Gog is going to bring a vast army with him. "You and all your troops and the many nations with you will go up, advancing like a storm; you will be like a cloud covering the land." (Ezekiel 38:9 NIV) The fact that Gog has many nations with him reinforces the fact that he is the leader of the world-wide Islamic Caliphate and can call on many Muslim nations to support him. The troops from these nations will be so numerous that they will cover the land like a cloud.

What will be Gog's purpose for attacking Israel? The Bible says that Gog will be coming to plunder and loot, to take gold and silver, and to take cattle and property.

> "Have you come to plunder? Have you gathered
> your hordes to loot, to carry off silver and gold,
> to take away livestock and goods and to seize
> much plunder?" (Ezekiel 38:13 NIV)

Gog will be treating Israel like they are occupiers on Islamic lands and that they have no right to exist and should be wiped off the face of the earth. This has constantly been the position of Islam since the inception of the nation of Israel in May of 1948. Gog will reinforce this position to the extreme and will order the Muslim nations under his Caliphate to destroy the nation of Israel.

The thing that Gog and his massive army never counted on is the Lord's reaction to their invasion of His land to destroy His people. Gog will be shocked and terrified when the Lord intervenes to stop Gog and his army where they stand. The Lord will tolerate many things that people do, but He will not tolerate the total and wanton destruction of His people that have been gathered out of the nations into His land. The Lord is going to be furious with the invading army foolish enough to attack the land of His chosen people. Gog and his army are going to be practically wiped out by the onslaught of the Lord in His anger. The Bible makes this clear in the following verse:

> This is what will happen in that day: When Gog attacks the land of Israel, my hot anger will be aroused, declares the Sovereign Lord. In my zeal and fiery wrath I declare that at that time there shall be a great earthquake in the land of Israel. The fish of the sea, the birds of the air, the beasts of the field, every creature that moves along the ground, and all the people on the face of the earth will tremble at my presence. The mountains will be overturned, the cliffs will crumble and every wall will fall to the ground. (Ezekiel 38:18-20 NIV)

The Lord is going to be furious with Gog and his armies and will act to destroy them by supernatural intervention from Heaven. First the Bible tells us there is going to be a cataclysmic earthquake—one so gigantic it will be felt by all people on the face of the earth.

This is not going to be a typical regional earthquake, but will be a worldwide earthquake. No one will be safe from this earthquake. It will impact "all the people on the face of the earth" and every fish, bird and creature on the face of the earth. It's as if our Lord is shaking the world to try to get our attention and to demonstrate that He is the one that is ultimately in control of our world. Gog will not be allowed to be successful in his endeavors. The way the Lord accomplishes this feat is just as alarming.

The Lord will use supernatural intervention to destroy Gog and all but one sixth of his massive army. The Lord marshals His weapons of destruction to accomplish His purpose.

The destructive elements will come from the sky and will pummel the earth and mountains where Gog's hordes are massing for their attack. The Bible tells us this in the following verse:

> I will execute judgment upon him with plague and bloodshed; I will pour down torrents of rain, hailstones and burning sulfur on him and on his troops and on the many nations with him. (Ezekiel 38:22 NIV)

What exactly are the rain, hailstones and burning sulfur referred to in this verse? The Lord is not talking about the normal rain we are familiar with. Instead, what is being described is a more appropriate description of meteorites and volatile materials falling from the skies and igniting a conflagration that ensues. This is confirmed later when the Lord says He will send fire on Magog. "I will send fire on Magog and on those who live in safety in the coastlands, and they will know that I am the Lord." (Ezekiel 39:6 NIV)

The Caliphate of Gog and all but one sixth of his massive army are going to be destroyed when the Lord moves to protect Israel from their onslaught.

> Son of man, prophesy against Gog and say: "This is what the Sovereign Lord says, I am against you, O Gog, chief prince of Meshech and Tubal. I will turn you around and drag you along. I will bring you from the far north and send you against the mountains of Israel. Then I will strike your bow from your left hand and make your arrows drop from your right hand. On the mountains of Israel

you will fall, you and all your troops and the nations with you." (Ezekiel 39:1-4 NIV)

Gog is going to be killed when he leads his forces against Israel in the Gog/Magog Battle described in the Bible. Fire falling from the sky will destroy many of Gog's forces. After this decisive intervention by the Lord, the Israeli Defensive forces will locate the body of Gog and will bury Gog and his hordes in the Valley of Hamon Gog.

> On that day I will give Gog a burial place in Israel, in the valley of those who travel east toward the Sea. It will block the way of travelers, because Gog and all his hordes will be buried there. So it will be called the valley of Hamon Gog. (Ezekiel 39:11 NIV)

The army of Gog was so huge it will take the people of Israel seven months to bury all of them. "For seven months the house of Israel will be burying them in order to cleanse the land." (Ezekiel 39:12 NIV) Even after the seven months of burying the hordes of Gog, Israel will have to permanently employ people to bury those who are found afterward.

> Men will be regularly employed to cleanse the land. Some will go throughout the land and, in addition to them, others will bury those that remain on the ground. At the end of seven months they will begin their search. As they go through the land and one of them sees a human bone, he will set up a marker beside it until the gravediggers have buried it in the Valley of Hamon Gog. And so they will cleanse the land. (Ezekiel 39:14-16 NIV)

The Muslim world has just suffered another tremendous defeat. Their leader of the Caliphate, Gog, is dead—but when he was alive he brought war to the world on an unprecedented level. His Caliphate may have been relatively short lived, but the damage he was able to accomplish will leave the world reeling. Just how damaging was Gog? How much destruction was accomplished when he was alive? That is exactly what we are going to look at next.

CHAPTER FIFTEEN
THE LEGACY OF GOG

Gog is going to leave a lasting imprint on the landscape of the entire world. He will fundamentally change many things during the time he is in power. His reign is so climactic that it begs the following question. Is Gog portrayed in any other area of the Bible beside the references in Ezekiel? Is he the same person as the antichrist? Let's dig a little deeper in the Bible and see what further insights we can gain with our examination.

In Ezekiel, Gog is characterized as a leader with a "bow" in his left hand. (Ezekiel 39:3) Is there any other place in the Bible that refers to a leader with a "bow" in his hand? There is another place in Scripture that describes a person with a bow in his hand. It is found in Revelation. Let's take a look at that verse:

> I watched as the Lamb opened the first of the seven seals. Then I heard one of the four living creatures say in a voice like thunder, "Come!" I

> looked and there before me was a white horse! Its rider held a bow, and he was given a crown, and he rode out as a conqueror bent on conquest. (Revelation 6:1-2 NIV)

Let's take a closer look at the symbols employed so we can understand what this verse is trying to tell us. First, this Scripture describes a rider on a "white horse." The white horse is symbolic of leadership. We find this reference in Revelation when Jesus Christ is depicted as coming from heaven riding upon a white horse. (Revelation 19:11) The leader riding on the white horse with a bow in his hand is a leader of a false religion that is trying to conquer the world. He is given a crown—which denotes his symbol of supreme leadership. This is exactly what will happen when Gog is given the overall leadership of the Muslim world—this happens when he is made the caliph of the Islamic Caliphate. He is given complete control over all things Islamic. He will then proceed to lead his Muslim forces in a forced subjugation of the entire world.

The leader depicted as having a bow in his left hand fits Gog perfectly. No other leader in end-times prophecies is described as having a bow in his left hand. The leader described in the first seal of Revelation is none other than Gog. He is the leader on the white horse and is one of the four horsemen of the Apocalypse. He goes forth bent on conquering the world. The natural consequences of his actions are described by the other three horsemen of the Apocalypse.

The second horseman is described as riding a fiery red horse. He is described as unleashing war on a global scale upon the world.

When the Lamb opened the second seal, I heard the second living creature say "Come!" Then another horse came out, a fiery red one. Its rider was given power to take peace from the earth and to make men slay each other. To him was given a large sword. (Revelation 6:3-4 NIV)

Gog's desire to rule the entire world will unleash war like we have not seen since the previous two World Wars. Peace will be taken from the earth when Gog instructs his followers to carry out jihad on all nations that will not follow his leadership. He has a huge advantage in carrying out this war because he already has a tremendous number of followers already imbedded in the nations of the world ready to follow all of the orders coming from the leader of the Caliphate. Just because ISIS was destroyed previously in the Psalm 83 War does not mean that there is any shortage of radical Islamic followers ready to carry out jihad on a global scale. Gog will tap into the network of those believers to unleash war on all nations.

The third horseman is a natural result of the first two. He unleashes famine on a global scale. When people are worried about being killed in a war, they don't plant and grow crops like they normally would. Also, what limited crops are planted can be destroyed when the war continues without ceasing. Consequently, it is going to cost a whole day's wages just to be able to buy what a person needs for food for that day. We are told this in the following verses:

> When the lamb opened the third seal, I heard the third living creature say "Come!" I looked, and there before me was a black horse! Its rider was holding a pair of scales in his hand. Then I heard what sounded like a voice among the four living creatures, saying, "A quart of wheat for a day's

wages, and three quarts of barley for a day's wages, and do not damage the oil and wine." (Revelation 6:5-6 NIV)

Famine will overwhelm the entire world. There will not be enough food to go around and many people will die from lack of food during the time of war Gog unleashes on the world. It will be a horrible time to endure.

The last horseman summarizes some of our worst fears. This rider rides a pale horse which is indicative of death. In fact, the rider's name is death. He has the power to unleash death on a global scale from war, famine and plague; and by the wild beasts of the earth. He is described in the following manner:

When the Lamb opened the fourth seal, I heard the voice of the fourth living creature say, "Come!" I looked, and there before me was a pale horse! Its rider was named Death, and Hades was following close behind him. They were given power over a fourth of the earth to kill by sword, famine and plague, and by the wild beasts of the earth. (Revelation 6:7-8)

One of the most disturbing things about this description is the fact that one fourth of the world's population will be killed during this time. The current world's population is 7.3 billion people. That means that a little over 1.8 billion people are going to die during the time when the horsemen are released. They are going to die during the war that is unleashed, the famine that takes place, and the plagues that are going to result from these activities. The world's arsenals contain many examples of biological weapons, and it is almost certain that some of these biological weapons will be used in this war. We may see examples of horrendous diseases rampaging across the planet—many of them engineered to kill as many people as possible and all of them without viable vaccines to treat them except to the very few that release these diseases. If there are vaccines for these diseases, there are not enough vaccines to treat everyone in the population. It becomes easier to see how so many millions of people can die.

The legacy of Gog is going to be one of tremendous destruction before he is killed in the Gog/Magog War. Let's review the points we have just made.

Gog is the leader depicted in the Bible as having a bow in his left hand. He fits the description of the rider on the white horse with a bow in his hand that is the first horseman of the Apocalypse. The horsemen depict a natural series of events when war is unleashed on the entire world. Here are the descriptions of the four horsemen:

1. The rider on a white horse with a bow in his left hand is a leader and a conqueror bent on the conquest of the entire world.

2. The rider on the fiery red horse takes peace from the earth and unleashes war on a global scale.

3. The rider on the black horse unleashes a worldwide famine. Food will become so scarce that it will take an entire day's wages just to get enough to survive for one day.

4. The pale horse has a rider named death that unleashes death by the sword, famine and

plague and by the wild beasts of the earth.
One fourth of the world's population will be
killed by the onslaught of the four horsemen.
In today's population terms, that means that
over 1.8 billion people are going to die.

Gog's legacy will be one of tremendous death and destruction during his reign as leader of the Islamic Caliphate. He will be responsible for the deaths of more people than all of the previous world's despots combined. It is little wonder that he is assigned a place of death on the mountains of Israel when he leads a coalition of nations to attack Israel. The bow of war will be struck out of his left hand and he will die because of the hell he has unleashed on earth.

Gog is not the antichrist because he is **killed** and buried in the valley of Hamon Gog in Israel. (Ezekiel 39:11) The antichrist's fate is entirely different than Gog's fate. The antichrist is cast **alive** into a lake of fire burning with brimstone. (Revelation 19:20) The two cannot be the same person because of this fact. We will examine the characteristics of the antichrist later but next we need to discuss some of the things unleashed upon the world during the reign of Gog.

CHAPTER SIXTEEN
WHAT GOG UNLEASHES IN THE WORLD

Gog will ascend to world power during a time of chaos rampaging across the earth. One of the most troubling things Gog does is unleash a "spirit of destruction" during his leadership of the Islamic Caliphate. This spirit of destruction will manifest itself in many different ways. Certainly the release of biologically engineered diseases will be one way destruction on a massive scale will be accomplished. The release of genetically engineered Ebola, smallpox and flu viruses like H1N1 would be catastrophic to the world and will result in the deaths of millions of people. There is no way to effectively stop these diseases with the resources on hand; and once they are released they will burn through the world's population until most of the people exposed to them die. The people contracting these diseases will have to be isolated as much as possible to limit the spread of the outbreak until the pandemic runs its course and is slowly controlled.

There is another way forces of destruction will be unleashed on the unsuspecting world during this time of chaos. There are forces in the world today that are trying to release demonic hordes in the world. Most people would never suspect one of the places trying to accomplish this feat. It is located in Switzerland near the border with France. The town is called Pouilly, and before this town had its modern name it was called Apolliacum by the Romans. It was there that a temple dedicated to Apollo was established. Apollo was a variant of the name Apollyon, a Greek deity of "death and pestilence."

What is most disturbing is not what happened in ancient times at this site, but what it happening currently at this location. Located just under the site dedicated to Apollyon, the god of death and pestilence, lies Cern or the Large Hadron Collider. The Large Hadron Collider is the largest machine in the world and is the world's largest and most powerful particle accelerator. It is here that particles are accelerated nearly to the speed of light along a 27 kilometer ring of superconducting magnets buried 300 feet beneath the surface of the ground.[39]

CERN Large Hadron Collider located in Switzerland under the Site Dedicated to Apollyon

---

39   Cern Document Server, "The Large Hadron Collider," http://home.cern./topics/large-hadron-collider.

The experiments carried on at this site are some of the most complex and dangerous experiments ever conducted on the face of the earth. Particles are accelerated to nearly the speed of light and then smashed into each other using vast amounts of energy. Some in the scientific community, after seeing the results of the experiments conducted there, have argued that these experiments threaten humanity's existence.

The man in charge of the Large Hadron Collider, CERN Chief Sergio Bertolucci, has not calmed fears when he made the following comments in a public interview, "We are going to open a doorway at CERN and we may send something through it and something may come back to us."[40]

Dancing Shiva Doing the Dance of Destruction in Front of the CERN LHC Building

Chief Bertolucci seems to be acknowledging the fact that the real purpose of the CERN collider is to open a portal or

40   Mac Slavo, "They're Looking For The Voice of God-Tom Horn Explains The Dangers of CERN Particle Experiments," 21 October 2015, http://www.prison-planet.com/they're-looking-for-the-voice-of-god-tom-horn-explains-the-dangers-of-cern-particle-experiments.

gateway to another dimension, and then see what comes through the portal. This is dangerous almost to the point of insanity. Many of the scientists working on this project know that what they are doing could unleash dangerous forces beyond our comprehension. They freely admit this—in fact they have prominently displayed a statue of Shiva doing the dance of destruction, the Nataraj, in the front of the building housing the Large Hadron Collider.

The scientists at CERN know what they are doing even if they don't disclose this information to the public. The logo that represents their research is a stylistic 666 emblem that they say represents the Hadron Collider. Why would any true scientific organization choose the 666 emblem and have the deity Shiva doing a dance of destruction in front of their building if they did not know that their work could open a portal or gateway into another dimension that allows demonic forces to ascend through this portal onto the earth? They are actively trying to make this happen with their experiments.

When the Large Hadron Collider is powered up to full power, there is so much energy coursing through the circular pathway of the collider that any mishap could be truly catastrophic. No one knows what can truly happen, but it is very curious that the Bible has something to say about Apollyon and what happens when he arises from the abyss onto the face of the earth.

> When he opened the Abyss, smoke rose from it like the smoke from a gigantic furnace. The sun and sky were darkened by the smoke from the Abyss. And out of the smoke locusts came down upon the earth and were given power like that of scorpions of the earth. They were told not

to harm the grass of the earth or any pant or tree, but only those people who did not have the seal of God on their foreheads...They had as king over them the angel of the Abyss, whose name in Hebrew is Abaddon, and in Greek, **Apollyon**. (Revelation 9:2-5, 11 NIV, (Bold letters mine)

To think that people are actually striving to make this happen at a site dedicated to Apollyon (the CERN Large Hadron Collider) is almost mind boggling. From what we read in Revelation, demonic forces are going to ascend out of the abyss and cause untold havoc upon the face of the earth. Something is going to happen at CERN to release them.

Some of the scientists that have worked at CERN have been so troubled by the experiments going on there that they have left the project and will not continue working at a site actively pursuing such a dark agenda. It is unknown when the people working at CERN will be able to open this portal and release the demonic hordes being held in check at this point in time. They insist that their work will give them insights as to the nature of the universe through their work on particle physics. They may have no idea what dark forces are going to be unleashed with the successful operation of their device. They may think they know, but the full implications of what they have done may come too late for them to do anything about it. They are continuing on with an agenda that releases chaos into the world.

The "chaos" or "age of destruction agenda" fostered by the advent of Gog will not abate but will grow stronger during the days of Gog. This will also be a time of great deception when people will not know what to believe. One of the actions we have postulated will be carried out by Gog is the attack on Rome and the assassination of the pope. This was predicted by different prophecies that the Catholic Church is completely familiar with—the Prophecy of the Popes and the Third Secret of Fatima. What happens next after the Islamic Caliphate under the direction of Gog accomplishes this feat?

Muslim forces are going to continuously occupy the Vatican and will not allow the election of another pope. They do not want another religious organization to challenge the leadership of the Caliphate—so there can never be another pope elected in the Vatican. Who then will lead the Catholic Church?

Gog and his Muslim Caliphate will have the perfect answer to this question—at least perfect in their own minds. The Islamic Caliphate will say that the long promised Messiah has at last appeared in Israel and that those in the Catholic Church and other Christian religions should follow the new Messiah.

THE APPEARANCE OF THE FALSE PROPHET

Someone will appear in Israel and will say that they are the long awaited Messiah. Not only will this person say he is the Messiah, but he will be able to convince many Rabbis in the Jewish community of this fact. Does this scenario sound far-fetched or completely improbable to you? It is happening right now in the year 2016.

The prophecy of the return of the false Messiah is found in the Kabbalistic work of the Zohar. The Kabbalah is an esoteric method and discipline of thought that originated in Judaism and has undertones from the occult. The Zohar is the foundational text for Kabbalistic thought. It is important to emphasize the following fact. The person making his appearance in Israel is not Jesus Christ returning again the second time, but a false Messiah that comes to deceive the Jewish people. He will be very convincing. He will point to various things the Rabbis in Israel have been looking for and convince them he is their long awaited Messiah. He will use various things written in the Zohar as his proof that he is their Messiah. It might be helpful to look at one of the passages written that the false Messiah will highlight as his verification of authenticity. It is found in the following text of the Zohar:

> All the kings of the world shall assemble in the great city of Rome. And the Holy One, blessed be He, will shower fire and hail and meteoric stones upon them, until they are wiped out from the world. And only those kings who did not go to Rome will remain in the world. And they shall return and wage other wars. During this time, the King Messiah will declare himself throughout the whole world and many nations will gather around him together with many armies from all corners of the world. And all the children of Yisrael will assemble together in their places.[41]

It is uncanny how this text refers to the destruction of an enclave in Rome consisting of kings and religious leaders, and how they are destroyed. This is very similar to the Third Secret of Fatima that predicts the destruction in Rome and the death of the pope. What is truly remarkable is the fact that the false Messiah makes his appearance official at the time of this catastrophe. He appears on the

---

41   Rav Shimon Bar. Commentary by Yehuda Ashlag. Edited and compiled by Rabbi Michael Berg, "The Zohar: the First Ever Unabridged English Translation with Commentary," (23 Volume Set) Vol. 3: Lech lecha Vayera (Los Angeles: Kabbalah Centre Intl, 2003), p. 486. Google Books link Quoted here.

world stage before this to make himself known to the religious leaders (the Rabbis) in Israel.

There are hints in the Zohar that 2012-2016 is the time frame that he will begin appearing to the rabbis. This is based on some esoteric symbols and information found in their predictions. It is believable enough that many are convinced that the year 2016 holds special significance in the predictions of the Messiah.

These predictions are taken so seriously that some important rabbis in Israel are telling their followers that the Messiah will appear any day now. They say he began appearing to a select few individuals in 2012, and he will make his presence more fully known in 2016. For example, here is what some of the important Rabbis are saying.

The Rabbi Chaim Kanievsky, one of the most influential leaders in mainstream Ultra-Orthodox Judaism, has said that the coming of the Messiah is imminent.[42] He began this message in 2015 and has become more adamant in his prediction with the arrival of 2016. He is encouraging Jews to make it home to Israel and soon as possible and has told his students not to leave Israel because the Messiah will be coming soon.

Another important leader, Rabbi Yosef Berger, one of the rabbis in charge of King David's Tomb, has completed a Torah scroll that is to be presented to the Messiah when he makes his appearance. He completed this scroll as rapidly as he could, because he said there is not much time

---

42   Adam Eliyahu Berkowitz, "Leading Israeli Rabbi Says The Arrival Of The Messiah Is Imminent," *Breaking Israel News*, 3 July 2015, http://www.breakingisraelnews.com/44534/leading-israeli-rabbi-messiah-imminent-jewish-world/.

left before the Messiah makes himself known.[43] After this special Torah scroll was finished it was moved to King David's tomb. The ceremony was attended by some of the most influential rabbis in Israel including: Rabbi Yitchak Shtern, Rabbi Shalom Berger, Rabbi Reuven Elbaz (a leading Sephardic rabbi), Rabbi Dov Lior (the Chief Rabbi of Kiryat Arba), Rabbi Shalom Ber Sorotzkin (head of the Ateret Shlomo Yeshiva), and many others.

While all of the rabbis are honest men and sincere in their convictions, this is not the way that the Messiah is going to make himself known. In fact, Jesus even said this in his own words when he was alive on the earth. He said that he would be rejected by the Jewish people, and yet another would come in his own name and would be accepted by the rabbis and other religious leaders in Israel. We find that quotation in the Gospel of John:

> I have come in my Father's name, and you do not accept me, but if someone else comes in his own name, you will accept him. (John 5:43 NIV)

Those words are literally being fulfilled in Israel right now. When Jesus Christ does come again the second time, the whole world will know about it. You will not have to be an important rabbi or a special group of elite people with special privileges. If you are alive at that time, you will see Jesus Christ coming from heaven in the following manner:

> I saw heaven standing open and there before me was a white horse, whose rider is called Faithful

---

43   Adam Eliyahu Berkowitz, "Special Torah Scroll Written For Messiah Completed," *Breaking Israel News*, 22 March 2016, http://www.breakingisraelnews.com/64082/special-torah-scroll-written-messiah-completed-photos-jewish-world/.

and True. With justice he judges and makes war. His eyes are like blazing fire, and on his head are many crowns. He has a name written on him that no one knows but he himself. He is dressed in a robe dipped in blood, and name is the Word of God. The armies of heaven were following him, riding on white horses and dressed in fine linen, white and clean. Out of his mouth comes a sharp sword with which to strike down the nations. He will rule them with an iron scepter. He treads the winepress of the fury of the wrath of God Almighty. On his robe and on his thigh he has this name written: King of Kings, and Lord of Lords. (Revelation 19:11-16 NIV)

Jesus warned us that men would come saying that they are Christ or the promised Messiah, and that we should not believe them. He told us this specifically in many places in the New Testament. In the Gospel of Matthew He warned:

At that time if anyone says to you, "Look, here is the Christ!" or "There he is!" do not believe it. For false Christs and false prophets will appear and perform great signs and miracles to deceive even the elect—if that were possible. See, I have told you ahead of time. So if anyone tells you, "There he is, out in the desert," do not go out; or "Here he is, in the inner rooms," do not believe it. For as lightning that comes from the east is visible even in the west, so will be the coming of the Son of Man. (Matthew 24:23-27 NIV)

The Messiah that is revealing himself to the rabbis in Israel is the false Messiah. This false Messiah is a shill for the antichrist. He is not Jesus Christ, but an imposter masquerading as the Messiah. Gog has released a spirit of deception in the world, and the false Messiah is another fulfillment of that spirit of deception.

The purpose of the false Messiah is to be a pawn for the antichrist, and to tell all people that they must follow the antichrist to be saved. It will be the greatest lie ever told. Following this false Messiah will lead to your destruction. Stay as far away from him as you can and do not listen to anything he has to say—even if he performs miracles and signs to verify his word.

People are going to believe this man when he says he is the Messiah. There are three reasons this is going to happen and we will discuss those reasons in the next chapter.

CHAPTER SEVENTEEN
REASONS FOR THE GREAT DECEPTION

There are some very specific reasons people will believe so readily in the false Messiah when he makes his appearance. They are going to believe that the completion of the Psalm 83 War, and the Gog/Magog War, both where Islamic forces suffer catastrophic defeats, are the Battle of Armageddon. Most people are expecting only one major war in end-times prophecy scenario—and when any major war takes place they will think that the Battle of Armageddon has just happened.

What happens after the Battle of Armageddon takes place? Most people are expecting Jesus Christ to appear on the scene again in His Second Coming. Anyone who appears on the world scene after either of these climactic battles and claims he is Jesus Christ is going to be accepted with open arms. The false Messiah will fulfill what many people are expecting to happen after a major war in the Middle East—and many will suspend their unbelief and embrace him completely. When he performs miraculous signs, then any further doubts will be cast aside.

For this reason we must understand that there are three major wars in the nation of Israel's future. The Bible carefully details each of these wars. Each war has a purpose and follows a pattern of fulfillment from ancient times. These are the three wars in Israel's future:

1. The Psalm 83 War: the Caliphate of Abu Bakr al-Baghdadi and ISIS will be destroyed in this war.

2. The Gog/Magog War: the man known as Gog will take over the Caliphate and after several successes in battle will come against the nation of Israel with a massive army and be destroyed.

3. The Battle of Armageddon: we will discuss the major players in this war and how they come about in a latter chapter.

If you would like to learn more about these three wars, and the ancient pattern they fulfill you can read the book *Fifteen Days in September That Will Change the World* by Mark S. Hoffmeister available on Amazon.

The first reason for the great deception is that many people think any major war in the Middle East is the Battle of Armageddon. This means that people are looking for the wrong things because of their misperception of which war is taking place. The second reason for the great deception is because the rabbis in Israel are being deceived by an imposter. Because they rejected their true Messiah, the rabbis in Israel are looking for someone to come and claim to be their long-awaited Messiah. There is almost a frenzy of expectation built up at this current time with the tantalizing hints of appearance by the mysterious figure talked about in the Zohar. The religious leaders in Israel are almost desperate to make someone their promised Messiah. It would vindicate their rejection of Jesus Christ so many years ago. It will be an event devoid of victory when the false Messiah makes himself known to them. There will something "off" and "unsettling" when this man speaks to them—something not quite right—but since they will view him as their promised Messiah they will give him the benefit of the doubt in his early reign as their promised one.

Eventually, even the most ardent of supporters of the false Messiah will realize that they have made a terrible mistake and will move to correct their error. This mistake will come with a terrible price and the people of Israel will suffer greatly at the hands of the false Messiah. The false Messiah will be closely aligned with the office of the Caliphate and will become a tool in the hands of the Caliphate to manipulate the Jewish people. This false Messiah will tell Israel that the coming antichrist is the person they must acknowledge and follow. Just how much they suffer depends on how quickly they realize the gravity of their error.

The way that the nation of Israel is going to have to acknowledge their current error and the errors of the past is by saying something that Jesus Christ said they would have to say before he returns to defend them. In the Gospel of Matthew Jesus said that Israel would have to say the following before they see him again:

> For I tell you, you will not see me again until you say, "Blessed is he who comes in the name of the Lord." (Matthew 23:39 NIV)

This particular phrase comes out of Psalm 118 and is a place where Israel in national unity acknowledges that the Lord is their God and they will praise and exalt the Lord.

> Blessed is he who comes in the name of the Lord. From the house of the Lord we bless you. The Lord is God, and he has made his light shine upon us. With boughs in hand, join in the festal procession up to the horns of the altar. You are my God, and I will give you thanks; you are my God, and I will exalt you. Give thanks to the Lord, for he is good; his love endures forever. (Psalm 118:26-29 NIV)

Israel will have to shun the false Messiah and acknowledge Jesus Christ as their true Messiah before He comes back to defend them. The lies told by the false Messiah will cause deception and deceit to prosper in the land of Israel. This is the second reason for great confusion and deception in the land.

The third reason for the great deception results because of something that happens when the forces of Gog are being destroyed by supernatural intervention by the Lord. When Gog comes against the nation of Israel to destroy it something happens that changes everything on the face of the earth. It is a profound change in the way the Lord deals with people from the moment it happens until the Second Coming of the Lord. Nothing will be the same from this point on because something is removed from the earth as a time known as the "Day of the Lord" begins.

What is going to happen? What is going to be removed? What is the Day of the Lord?

A great earthquake that shakes the entire earth is going to happen. The people with the Holy Spirit residing within them are going to be removed from the earth. A time of judgment is going to begin—the Day of the Lord— and it begins with the great earthquake described in the Gog/Magog War.

These topics are so important that they deserve their own chapter. It is absolutely critical that everyone understands what is going to happen when these three events transpire. Let's discuss them now.

CHAPTER EIGHTEEN
THE EVENTS SURROUNDING THE GREAT EARTHQUAKE

One of the critical events that will happen with the destruction of the Gog/Magog army is an earthquake so large that it shakes the entire world. The earthquake is described by Ezekiel in the following manner:

> In my zeal and fiery wrath I declare that at that time there shall be a great earthquake in the land of Israel. The fish of the sea, the birds of the air, the beasts of the field, every creature that moves along the ground, and all the people on the face of the earth will tremble at my presence. The mountains will be overturned, the cliffs will crumble and every wall will fall to the ground. (Ezekiel 38:19-20 NIV)

Everything is going to be affected by this earthquake: the fish of the sea, the birds, the beasts of the field, every creature that moves on the earth, and all people on the face of the earth are going to shake because of this earthquake. This is not your typical regional earthquake, but an earthquake on a worldwide scale that has not been felt for many millennia. It is the Lord shaking the world to try to get our attention. We will set aside the mechanics of how this is accomplished for now. The important question becomes: Is this earthquake mentioned any other place in the Bible?

The answer is a resounding YES! This identical earthquake is mentioned in Revelation when the sixth seal is opened. This makes perfect sense because we have previously described how the appearance of Gog in his role as the rider on the white horse unleashes the first four seals of Revelation—the Four Horsemen of the Apocalypse. Let's take a look at the great earthquake described in Revelation:

> I watched as he opened the sixth seal. There was a great earthquake. The sun turned black like sackcloth made of goat hair, the whole moon turned blood red, and the stars in the sky fell to earth, as late figs drop from a fig tree when shaken by a strong wind. (Revelation 6:12-13 NIV)

This earthquake is called the "great earthquake" in both the Gog/Magog passages and the description in Revelation. They both describe destruction that is felt and seen around the world. The description in Revelation is chilling because it foretells destruction that is so powerful that the dust and debris in the air blackens the sun in broad daylight. The moon is turned to the color of blood by the same destructive debris in the air. Clearly we can conclude from this description that a day of destruction has begun.

When the great earthquake strikes, it will herald the start of a time when great destruction will ravage the earth. This is a time period that is going to be known as the Day of the Lord. What may be surprising to many is the fact that the destruction during the Day of the Lord will be orchestrated by the Lord. The Day of the Lord initiates the time of the end. What happens before the Day of the Lord begins?

If we examine the Scriptures carefully, in the seventh chapter of Revelation, two things are going to happen before destruction is allowed to come upon the earth. First 144,000 people from the house of Israel are going to be sealed in their foreheads for service to the Lord. And secondly, immediately after that sealing, a great multitude of ethnically diverse people, from every nation, all speaking a variety of different languages; are going to appear in heaven before the throne of Jesus.

Who are these people? Let's take a look at what the Scripture says so we can get clues that will help us identify them.

> After this I looked and there before me was a great multitude that no one could count, from every nation, tribe, people and language, standing before the throne and in front of the Lamb. They were wearing white robes and were holding palm branches in their hands. (Revelation 7:9 NIV)

This is a vast amount of people that suddenly appears in heaven, which no man could number. They are from every nation on the earth, from every people, and they speak a variety of different languages. The apostle John seems shocked by their appearance in heaven since they seemed to come out of nowhere. He questions who these people are and where they came from? He is told the following in response to this question.

> These are they who have come out of the great tribulation; they have washed their robes and made them white in the blood of the Lamb. (Revelation 7:14 NIV)

The term, "come out of the great tribulation," indicates a time when the tribulation the church has normally endured is greatly intensified, and their sudden appearance represents an escape for this group of people. This would indicate that these people are escaping a time of great destruction, and are being protected and brought home. They are being protected by the Lord from a time when devastation and great tribulation is unleashed on the earth. This is what was promised by the rapture. This is the Lord's love and protection manifesting for those who have the Holy Spirit within them.

THE RAPTURE

These people standing before the throne of Jesus Christ are those raptured from the earth. Many have said that this group represents the martyred saints described in the fifth seal of Revelation. There is an important reason why this group cannot be the saints that have been killed for their testimony of Jesus. The people in the group that appears suddenly in heaven are given palm branches to hold in their hands. This means that they are not spirits like the Christians murdered in the fifth seal. The saints that have been killed have spiritual bodies and have not been resurrected yet—therefore they don't have actual physical hands with which they can hold things. Only after they are resurrected will they have the ability to physically hold things. This passage perfectly describes those that have been raptured from the earth and are now present with the Lord before His throne. **This group are those raptured from the earth.**

Before we continue, there needs to be some points of clarification on the rapture. One point that has never really been clarified before is why the rapture takes place. Yes we were promised the rapture and yes we are being provided a means of escape from the wrath of God—but why exactly are people removed from the earth before the judgment of the Lord takes place?

Through all my years of research no one has ever adequately explained why the rapture has to take place before the judgment of the Lord falls on the earth.

There is a very specific reason for the rapture. It has to do with a specific characteristic of the people being raptured. Those that are raptured have the gift of the Holy Spirit within them. The Holy Spirit dwells within them to the point that the Holy Spirit is an integral part of who that person is. The Holy Spirit is part of their essential being to the point that they are indistinguishable from the Holy Spirit in their actions. It doesn't mean they are perfect and without faults and sin, but the Holy Spirit guides and directs their actions representing Jesus Christ here on the earth acting through them. **The Lord cannot exercise judgment on Himself, and those with the Holy Spirit within them must be removed before judgment can take place. This is the reason for the rapture.**

With this concept in mind, we must correct some commonly misused terminology. The term, "The Rapture of the

Church," is the wrong terminology. It implies that if you are a member of a church then you will be raptured. The debate then becomes whether you are a true Christian or not a true Christian. All of this debate and mincing about the details of a true Christian is a distraction from the real issue. That is not the definitive point—it's whether you have the Holy Spirit within you that really matters.

Any person in any church that acknowledges Jesus Christ as their Savior can have the free gift of the Holy Spirit within them. All they have to do is ask for the Holy Spirit to guide and direct their lives each day in prayer. Let me caution you right now though. The gift of the Holy Spirit comes with a price. You have to give up all your secret sins; you have to give up all those things that are more important to you than Jesus Christ, you have to give up your head-strong ways where you do things your own way regardless of what the Lord is telling you to do, and you have to be willing to repent and say that you are a sinner and acknowledge that Jesus Christ is the only way which you will ever get to heaven.

People may argue all day whether they are a true Christian or not—but those that have the Holy Spirit within them are easy to recognize. They stand apart from most people because care and concern for others is manifest in many of the things they do. The Lord told us just how important the Holy Spirit is in our lives when He warned us of the following. **There are those in danger of missing the rapture because they do not have the Holy Spirit within them.** Jesus gave us specific examples of how this could happen.

- ▶ In the Parable of the Ten Virgins (Matthew 25:1-12), Jesus related an example of ten virgins who want to go to be with the bridegroom (Christ).

They were spiritually pure (virgins-members of His church) but some of them did not have the Holy Spirit within them (represented by the oil for their lamps). The foolish ones without the oil (the Holy Spirit) in their lamps were shut out when He came for them (the rapture). The Lord says He never knew them. The foolish virgins missed the rapture because they did not have the Holy Spirit within them.

▶ In Matthew, Jesus cites the example of people coming to Him and saying Lord, Lord and then listing all of the things that they have done that should qualify them for His Kingdom. This included prophesying, casting out devils, and doing many wonderful works. (Matthew 7:21-23) When these people finish their list of good works, Jesus confesses that He never knew them—much like the foolish virgins. They had never cultivated a relationship with Him and did not do as He asked of them. You get that guidance and direction from the Holy Spirit. These people were shocked that they were not automatically granted entry into the kingdom of heaven. Having the Holy Spirit within them was far more important than they ever knew.

▶ In the letters to the seven churches in Revelation (Revelation chapters 2 and 3), several of the churches were warned they were in danger of having their churches removed or going into the tribulation if they did not change their ways. Some of the churches were distracted from a relationship with Jesus where He guides their actions through the Holy Spirit

because of what they were doing or allowing
in their churches. They had left their first love
(Jesus) and were concentrating on other things
(Ephesus). They allowed Satan to infiltrate
their church with false doctrines (Pergamos).
They were overcome with fornication and false
doctrines (Thyatira). They were not watching
and not prepared for Jesus coming for them
(Sardis). And another church was apathetic to
the point that the Holy Spirit could not direct
any of their actions (Laodicea). One church was
different from the others (Philadelphia) because
it had an open door placed before it (rapture)
and was told that they would be kept from
the hour of temptation (tribulation) that would
come on the whole world.

Each of the churches was warned because one day the
Holy Spirit is going to be withdrawn from the world. The
Holy Spirit came to the world at a specific time during the
early church at the day of Pentecost (Acts 2:1-4) and has
been available to anyone that accepts Jesus Christ as their
Savior. The Holy Spirit will leave the world at a very specific
time also.

The Apostle Paul told us that there was a secret power of
lawlessness at work in the world, but the one who holds it
back (Holy Spirit) would continue to hold it back until He is
taken out of the way (2 Thessalonians 2:7). Only the Holy
Spirit can restrain lawlessness and the Holy Spirit is going
to leave the earth during the rapture. When He leaves, He
will be taking those that have the gift of the Holy Spirit
inside them with Him. The rapture removes those with the
Holy Spirit within them from the earth, leaving the world

vulnerable to the destructive events that come during the judgment that follows.

Prior to our discussion on the rapture, we were talking about the great earthquake and the appearance in heaven of the great multitude. These vast numbers of people appear in heaven before the devastation of the great earthquake is allowed to take place. After these people appear in heaven, the destructive events heralded by the day of the Lord, starting with the great earthquake begin.

Those raptured appear in Heaven, and the seventh chapter of Revelation says that this happens before the devastation of the great earthquake. "Hurt not the earth, neither the sea, nor the trees, till we have sealed the servants of our God in their foreheads." (Revelation 7:3)

The great earthquake represents the beginning of the Day of the Lord judgments against the earth, and many (those having the Holy Spirit within them) are going to escape the wrath of God displayed in the Day-of-the-Lord judgments. After the rapture, the Day of the Lord begins.

Let's summarize some of the things we have said to keep these concepts clear in our minds.

- ► Gog takes over the Islamic Caliphate after the destruction of ISIS and locates his Caliphate in the nation of Turkey.

- ► Gog is the rider on the white horse that unleashes the four horsemen of the Apocalypse scenario in Revelation.

- ► With the Islamic nations supporting him, Gog has several victories over other nations including the Vatican. He releases war on the entire world and 1.8 billion people are killed.

▶ Gog prepares a massive army to destroy the nation of Israel. The army is so large that Gog feels it is impossible to defeat his army. His army is in the process of attacking Israel when the Lord intervenes to protect Israel.

▶ A global earthquake shakes the entire world.

▶ The world-wide earthquake during Gog's attack is the same great earthquake described as the sixth seal in the Book of Revelation.

▶ Before the great earthquake is allowed to take place, 144,000 of the house of Israel are sealed and set apart to serve the Lord.

▶ Before the great earthquake is allowed to take place, true Christians with the Holy Spirit within them are raptured and appear in heaven, to escape persecution and death and to be protected from the destruction and devastation when the wrath of God is unleashed during the Day of the Lord.

▶ The Holy Spirit withdraws from the world and no longer restrains the secret power of lawlessness and destruction.

▶ The world enters a time of judgment, not grace.

▶ The Day of the Lord begins and a period of intense deception, destruction and devastation commences.

The timing we have just discussed places the rapture before the appearance of the antichrist. There are many that say the rapture of the church does not occur until after the antichrist has appeared on the world scene. They base this assumption on a Scripture found in Second Thessalonians. Let's examine this Scripture and see what the real meaning behind it is and see if we can dispel the confusion. Here's the Scripture:

> Now we beseech you, brethren, by the coming of our Lord Jesus Christ, and by our gathering together unto him. (2 Thessalonians 2:1)

Let's stop right here for a moment and examine what has been said. The term, the "coming of our Lord Jesus Christ" refers to the Second Coming of Jesus when He comes to the earth for the second time. This event is depicted in the Scriptures in the nineteenth chapter of Revelation. The other term in this verse, "our gathering together unto him" refers to the rapture which takes place at the sixth seal of Revelation, chapter six. Paul is telling us in this verse not to confuse the Second Coming of Jesus Christ with the rapture—they are two separate and very distinct events.

Let's continue to analyze what has been said:

> That ye be not soon shaken in mind, or be troubled, neither by spirit, nor by word, nor by letter as from us, as that the day of Christ is at hand. (2 Thessalonians 2:2)

It's important to note what has just been said here. The term, "the day of Christ" is a reference to the Second

Coming of Jesus Christ. This point is made in the first chapter of Second Thessalonians.

> And to you who are troubled rest with us, when the Lord Jesus shall be revealed from heaven with his mighty angels. (2 Thessalonians 1:7)

This is clearly talking about the Second Coming of Jesus Christ when He will be revealed from heaven. The term "in that day" is used later on in this verse in reference to the Second Coming of Jesus. (2 Thessalonians 1:10) "In that day" is a clear reference to the Second Coming of Christ. It might seem that this point is being overemphasized, but it is critical to understand what the Scripture is actually saying. The term "in that day" is a clear reference to the Second Coming of Jesus, it doesn't refer to the Day of the Lord or any other day.

The reason this is important is because of what the rest of the Scripture says:

> Let no man deceive you by any means: for that day [the Second coming of Jesus Christ] shall not come except there comes a falling away first, and that man of sin be revealed [the antichrist], the son of perdition; who opposeth and exalteth himself above all that is called God, or that is worshipped; so that he as God sitteth in the temple of God shewing himself that he is God. (2 Thessalonians 2:3-4)

What this Scripture is saying is that Jesus Christ will not come again in His Second Coming (Revelation 19) until the antichrist is revealed and there is a falling away in the church. Many have confused the term "in that day" with the Day of the Lord, and insist that the antichrist has to be revealed before the Day of the Lord comes. This is clearly not what the text in Thessalonians says. It is saying the antichrist must be revealed before the Second Coming, and should not be confused with thinking the antichrist is going to be revealed before the destruction associated with the Day of the Lord begins. The Day of the Lord begins with the sixth seal great earthquake, and up until this point in time, the antichrist has not yet made his appearance on the world stage.

This places the rapture before the advent of the antichrist, and before the tremendous destruction that begins with the Day of the Lord.

Everything changes with the rapture and the great earthquake. The end of the world as we know it is beginning. Jesus will be removing His followers to be with Him, and because they have been removed from the earth, the protection bestowed upon the nations will be taken away. All the nations of the world will be vulnerable unlike anytime they have ever experienced. The protection afforded the nations because of the ones living in them will vanish along with those that are taken into heaven. It will truly be a time for hell to reign on earth.

And it all starts when the age of destruction begins.

CHAPTER NINETEEN
THE AGE OF DESTRUCTION RETURNS

One of the points that cannot be emphasized enough is just how much the Holy Spirit has been protecting us from. When the Holy Spirit withdraws from the earth, He withdraws His protection and restraining influence also. This leaves the earth and its remaining inhabitants vulnerable to all kinds of horrors. When the Holy Spirit leaves—the age of destruction is forestalled no longer.

Just how much has the Holy Spirit been protecting us from? From the time the Holy Spirit was given during the day of Pentecost after the death and resurrection of Jesus, until the time in the near future when the Holy Spirit withdraws from the earth along with the raptured saints, the earth has been protected from any major global catastrophes. Yes there have been many wars and localized tragic events like Tsunamis, earthquakes, volcanoes, hurricanes and tornadoes, but these have been restricted in their size and the scope of damage they can do. These restrictions are going to be removed after the Holy Spirit leaves the earth. Many are going to see destructive events that become global in nature and widespread in the areas that are affected.

We are given an example of this when we look at the destruction of Gog's army. One of the things that happen at this time is a global earthquake that strikes the earth. It affects every part of the earth and impacts every person on the face of the earth. The destruction of Gog's army represents a departure from the ordinary also. We are told that the Lord destroys Gog's army using weapons like hailstones (*barad*--more like meteorites or falling rocks) and burning sulfur that falls from the sky.

> I will execute judgment upon him with plague and bloodshed; I will pour down torrents of rain, hailstones and burning sulfur on him and on his troops and on the many nations with him. (Ezekiel 38:22 NIV)

When Magog is destroyed, it is literally burnt out of existence with fire falling from the sky. "I will send fire on Magog and on those who live in safety in the coastlands, and they will know that I am the Lord." (Ezekiel 39:6 NIV) This is a significant departure from what has happened before in the last two thousand years. This is more like Old Testament times when worldwide catastrophic events were more common. For example, the flood of Noah represents a near extinction level event that overcame the earth. This is what the Holy Spirit has been restraining on a global basis for almost two thousand years. **When mankind decides they don't want the Lord in their lives, and those with the Holy Spirit within them have been removed, the Lord will allow the full consequences of this rejection to overcome man.** The age of destruction known as the Day of the Lord will begin. It is a time of judgment and destruction and a time that no sane person would want to be involved in.

THE DAY OF THE LORD

The Day of the Lord has been described in many ways—all of them a picture of darkness, gloominess and a time when destruction overwhelms the earth. The Day of the Lord is a time of great destruction upon the earth. It is a time of judgment. It is a time signaling the end of the world and it all begins with a great earthquake.

The prophet Joel describes the Day of the Lord in the following way:

> Blow the trumpet in Zion; sound the alarm on my holy hill. Let all who live in the land tremble, for the day of the Lord is coming, it is close at hand. (Joel 2:1 NIV)

Notice how the inhabitants of the land tremble—signifying a great earthquake; and when this sign is given, the Day of the Lord is ready to start. The sign of an earthquake is reinforced later on in this same chapter when it says:

> Before them the earth shakes, the sky trembles, the sun and moon are darkened, and the stars no longer shine. (Joel 2:10 NIV)

Notice how similar this language is to the language used to describe the sixth seal when the great earthquake occurs in Revelation. (Revelation 6:12)

Joel is describing the agents the Lord will be using to carry out the destruction, and the agents being used will come as destruction from the Almighty.

> Alas for that day! For the day of the Lord is near;
> it will come like destruction from the Almighty."
> (Joel 1:15)

Joel describes the Day of the Lord as a day of darkness, gloominess, thick clouds, and a day when tremendous destruction is taking place:

> The day of the Lord is coming; it is close at hand,
> a day of darkness and gloom, a day of clouds
> and blackness. Like dawn spreading across the
> mountains, a large and mighty army comes, such
> as never of old nor ever will be in ages to come.
> Before them fire devours, behind them a flame
> blazes. Before them the land is like the Garden
> of Eden, behind them, a desert waste—nothing
> escapes them. (Joel 2:1-3 NIV)

The prophet Isaiah paints a vivid picture of what the Day of the Lord is like. He describes the Day of the Lord and points out that it is caused by the weapons the Lord has gathered from the end of heaven. These are the weapons used to cause the destruction wreaking havoc in the Day of the Lord:

> The Lord Almighty is mustering an army for war.
> They come from faraway lands, from the ends
> of the heavens, the Lord and the weapons of
> his wrath—to destroy the whole country. Wail

for the day of the Lord is near; it will come like destruction from the Almighty. Because of this, all hands will go limp, every man's heart will melt. Terror will seize them, pain and anguish will grip them; they will writhe like a woman in labor. They will look aghast at each other, their faces aflame. See, the day of the Lord is coming, a cruel day, with wrath and fierce anger—to make the land desolate and destroy the sinners within it. The stars of heaven and their constellations will not show their light. The rising sun will be darkened and the moon will not give its light. I will punish the world for its evil, the wicked for their sins. I will put an end to the arrogance of the haughty and will humble the pride of the ruthless. (Isaiah 13:4-11 NIV)

Again we see imagery of darkness and destruction, so much so that the sun and moon will be darkened and cannot be seen. People will not be able to see the stars either. This will most likely be from the clouds and smoke from the destruction taking place on the earth.

God's Word is filled with descriptions of the Day of the Lord, but let's look at another place where it is described in detail. This description is found in Zephaniah, and again a time of destruction and desolation is pointed out.

The great day of the Lord is near—near and coming quickly. Listen! The cry on the day of the Lord will be bitter, the shouting of the warrior there. That day will be a day of wrath, a day of distress and anguish, a day of trouble and ruin, a day of darkness and gloom, a day of clouds and blackness. (Zephaniah 1:14-15 NIV)

It is apparent from all these examples that the Day of the Lord is a day of destruction, thick clouds, darkness, and gloominess. It is a day that comes as destruction from the Lord, and starts with a great earthquake as we saw in Joel.

THE CAUSE OF THE DESTRUCTION

What could cause all of the destruction we are seeing we are seeing in the Day of the Lord judgments? What has been held back and is allowed to cause worldwide devastation once again?

We are given our first clue from a rather cryptic phrase in Isaiah. The prophet Isaiah when speaking of this destruction said that the Lord is gathering an army for this war, and they come from the "ends of the heavens." (Isaiah 13:4-5) What does that mean?

The phrase the "ends of the heavens" would imply something far out in space that rarely makes its appearance in our world. When it does appear, we can infer from the Day of the Lord passages that it causes tremendous destruction on the earth. What in the world could this possibly be?

To answer that question we need to look at a place no one would suspect an answer to come from. We need to look at an odd set of circumstances that pitted the Apache Indian Nation against the Vatican in a dispute over a mountain in Arizona. What in the world was this dispute?

The Apache Indian Nation brought a lawsuit against the Vatican when the Catholic Church wanted to construct a large binocular telescope atop Mt. Graham in Arizona—a sacred mountain in Apache lands. After much legal wrangling and intervention by congress on the side of the Vatican, the Catholic Church prevailed and built the world's largest infrared binocular telescope on Mt. Graham. The Vatican named this telescope an ominous and portentous name—they call it Lucifer. The Lucifer device is the world's most advanced binocular telescope and allows the Vatican to see objects in the heavens using the infrared spectrum. The infrared spectrum used by the Lucifer device is capable of tracking objects that cannot be seen in the normal light spectrum used by other telescopes.

The Lucifer telescope operated by the Vatican on Mt. Graham

What is absolutely unnerving is not the name the Vatican gave this telescope—Lucifer—but the fact that since its construction and start of operation, the Vatican has been tracking something coming toward the earth from the outer reaches of space. The Vatican has refused to comment on the object of their studies with this telescope, but word has leaked out from sources connected with the Vatican concerning the Lucifer telescope. Father Malachi Martin was a noted Catholic theologian and commented on the Art Bell program Coast to Coast one night why the Catholic Church was so heavily invested in things happening in deep space. His comments left the listeners to this program stunned. Father Martin said: "The mentality...amongst those who are at the ...highest levels of Vatican administration and geopolitics, know...what's going on in space, and what's approaching us..."[44]

What could Father Malachi Martin have been referring to? What is approaching us? While the Vatican observers have failed to comment, the website set up for the Lucifer device has been far more informative. The following inscription is found there:

NASA AND THE VATICAN'S INFRARED TELESCOPE CALLED [LUCIFER]—A German built, NASA and The Vatican owned and funded Infrared Telescope...for looking at NIBIRU/NEMESIS.[45]

Finally we are told what the Lucifer telescope is tracking in space. They are looking at and studying a planet called Nibiru or Nemesis, and sometimes referred to as Planet X. Perhaps a little background on Nibiru would be helpful.

For a long time there have been rumors of a mysterious planet with a highly elliptical orbit of 3600 years that infrequently comes into our solar system. It's a massive planet or small star system approximately ten times the size of earth with an orbit so highly elongated that it is rarely seen. It is also a very dark planet that is hard to see in the normal light spectrum. When it comes into our solar system it causes catastrophic disruptions to the planets in

44   Chris Putnam and Thomas Horn, *Exo-Vaticana* (Crane, MO: Defender, 2013), p. 21.
45   Ibid, p. 25.

our solar system and disorder that takes countless years to subside.

What is most destructive about this planet's onslaught through our solar system is the gravitational forces it exerts on any planet it comes close to. If it came near the earth, massive tidal forces would be generated that affect not only the oceans, but the crustal plates of the earth also. The gravitational pull of this gigantic planet passing nearby could cause oceanic tides several thousands of feet tall, and earthquakes of an almost unimaginable scale would rock the earth as it passes by our planet. Dormant volcanoes would become active again and blacken the sky with the massive amounts of ash thrown into the atmosphere. The destructive events that would overwhelm the earth would be almost incalculable.

Before we dismiss any appearance of this planet as being too outlandish to actually believe, we need to examine certain facts that are available to us. First of all, let's take a look at history and see if they are any hints that this massive planet has come by the earth in the past.

According to biblical scholars and geophysicists there was an event that happened many years ago that produced the exact effects we have just described. It was the biblical flood of Noah, and for all intents and purposes, this was an extinction level event where only a handful of people survived the encounter. The world was wiped out by floods of water sweeping across the continents leaving Noah and his family to repopulate the earth.

Could something like this ever happen again? Remember the Holy Spirit has been protecting us from catastrophic events of this nature from happening. With the Holy Spirit removed, there is no protection from catastrophic events like this. In fact, Jesus warned us that the end-times would be just like the days of Noah. (Matthew 24:37) Could he have been referring to the return of the destroying planet when he made this comparison? Since Christ said the times of Noah would be just like the times of the end, then it is safe to assume that a destroying planet could make its appearance once again. It is nearly impossible to read the book of Revelation and not come to the conclusion that the earth is going to be bombarded by catastrophic events consistent with the arrival of something from space. The debris captured in the destroying planet's orbit could be the cause of volatile materials falling to the earth and burning up trees and grass (Revelation 8:7), the burning mountain cast into the seas (Revelation 8:8), the star called Wormwood that makes the waters bitter (Revelation 8:10-11), and the darkness that envelopes the earth (Revelation 8:12).

The works of Immanuel Velikovsky, *Worlds in Collision*, and *Earth in Upheaval*, document the effects of this interplanetary visitor wreaking chaos on the planets of our solar system. Even after the destroying planet left our solar system, it disrupted the orbits of the planets so much that there were constant orbital perturbations that caused continued catastrophic interactions between the planets.

I would highly recommend the reader looking at the works of a biblical scholar named Donald Wesley Patten. He exhaustively documents the themes of catastrophic occurrences caused by the past and future appearance of the destroying planet in the Old Testament. His book is called *Catastrophism and the Old Testament* and in it he lists over 1000 instances of catastrophic language that paints the picture of the devastating interactions between the planets set in motion by the appearance of the destroying planet. Those themes dominate the Old Testament books of Amos, Exodus, Jonah, Joshua, Judges, Nahum, Job and especially the Book of Isaiah.[46]

The cause of the great earthquake and the great destruction we find portrayed in the pages of the Bible is consistent with another appearance of the destroying planet called Nibiru/Nemesis/Planet X coming in proximity with the planet Earth. It is coming again and the times will be just like the time of Noah.

The internet is rife with examples and stories about this planet and how it is going to make its appearance again soon. Much of this information is undependable and full of speculation. There is no way for the average person to know when this is going to happen again—and if you spend your time worrying about this event you have missed the point. Spend your time doing good for other people and seeking the guidance and direction of the Holy Spirit within you. Having the Holy Spirit within you will protect you from these times and will cause you to be engaged in the things that the Lord would have you do. Concentrate on those things and not the destruction looming on the horizon. The Lord will keep you and protect you.

We will need His protection, because along with the time of destruction, a time of deception and chaos will accompany the time of destruction.

---

46   Donald Wesley Patten, *Catastrophism and the Old Testament*, (Seattle, WA: Pacific Meridian Publishing Company, 1988) p. 94.

—

CHAPTER TWENTY
THE AGE OF DECEPTION AND TERROR

One salient fact that most of us may never have considered is just how much the Holy Spirit has been protecting us. Not only have we been shielded from the devastating events associated with a huge planet rampaging through our solar system and devastating the earth, but we have been protected from many of the things that want to do us harm.

We may have overlooked and been unaware of the fact that the Holy Spirit has protected us from far more things than we ever imagined. We've survived this long relatively unscathed because we have always had someone on our side that has constantly been looking out for us. This is no longer true when the Holy Spirit leaves. Nightmare scenarios that have haunted our dreams will be allowed to come to pass. Those who want nothing to do with the Lord and His protective Spirit will have their wishes granted. The restraining influence of the Holy Spirit will be withdrawn leaving people vulnerable to attack from many different realms. What form will these nightmares and attacks take? What great deception will be perpetrated on mankind?

Here are some possible answers:

- ► The issue of the existence of aliens and the alien phenomenon and deception will no longer be restrained. Some of the foremost researchers into the alien issue, such as the legendary French UFO researcher Dr. Jacques Vallee, have concluded that the appearance of aliens is more consistent with demonic entities assuming any form that gains them entry into our world. The alien phenomenon more closely resembles attributes of demonic manipulation than anything else.[47]

  However, there is no question about the highly advanced technology associated with this issue. Should the alien phenomenon be allowed to progress unrestrained, the current defensive measures deployed by all of the nations of the world will be no match for the technology brought against the earth. The forces behind the alien issue will deny God and propose that a super-race of highly intelligent immortal beings is responsible for mankind's existence. If you think that this scenario is highly improbable then you need to look more closely at Psalm 82. This Psalm describes God giving judgment to a great assembly of "gods." These gods are immortals that have come down to the earth and are responsible for great wickedness

---

47   Chris Putnam and Thomas Horn, *Exo-Vaticana*, (Crane, MO: Defender, 2013), p. 151.

and great deception on the earth. They "walk
about in darkness" when the "foundations
of the earth are shaken" [great earthquake].
These immortals cause such great wickedness
to flourish on the earth that their judgment
is that they are going to die like mere men.
"I said you are "gods"; you are all sons of the
Most High. But you will die like mere men; you
will fall like every other ruler." (Psalm 82:6-7
NIV) A group of super-intelligent immortals is
going to be on the earth deceiving men and
trying to get men to worship them. They will
fail eventually and die, but the deceit they bring
on man will be devastating. These forces will be
so convincing that the world and all the people
left in the churches after those with the Holy
Spirit have been raptured will fall away from the
truth of Jesus Christ in droves. If you would like
to read more about the alien deception and the
immortals coming to the earth in the days of
destruction and terror I would highly recommend
you read the book, *On the Path of the
Immortals*, by Thomas Horn and Chris Putnam.

► Another thing coming upon the earth during
the days of destruction was first talked about
in the Bible in Genesis chapter six. It says:
"There were giants in the earth in those days;
and also after that, when the sons of God came
in unto the daughters of men, and they bore
children to them, the same became mighty men
which were of old, men of renown." (Genesis
6:4) These giants were the offspring of fallen
angels and their interactions with women on
the earth. (Genesis 6:2) The giants were a

menace to all mankind and constantly sought to
destroy men. The fallen angels that created the
giants were engaged in genetic manipulation
that resulted in the corruption of almost the
entire genetic code of man. The God-inspired-
genetic code of man was in danger of being
completely corrupted by the interference of
these fallen angels. These angels were so
successful in changing the genetic code of man
and animals to the point that a form of "genetic
Armageddon" took place. Noah was one of
the only people on the face of the earth that
had regular human genetic code left. (Genesis
6:9) He and his family were saved on the ark
to preserve the original human genetic code
from which Jesus Christ would be born. The
giants were constantly killing men and were
condemned by God. The creators of the giants,
the fallen angels were bound by the Lord for
a period of seventy generations underneath
the earth. We are told this in the Book of
Enoch in chapter ten: "Bind them for seventy
generations underneath the earth." (Enoch
10:15) The Book of Enoch was referenced
in the Bible in both Jude and in the Psalms.
What is most troubling is the fact that the
giants are going to be unleashed upon the
earth once again "during the days of slaughter
and destruction." We are told this in Enoch
chapter fifteen: "The spirits of the giants shall
be like clouds, which shall oppress, corrupt,
fall, contend, and bruise upon earth. They
shall cause lamentation...for they come forth
during the days of slaughter and destruction."
(Enoch 15:9-10) When the giants are released

from their confinement once again, they will come forth during a time of destruction and slaughter and will kill all of the men that they can find. They will be a plague on all mankind. Those seventy generations of confinement will expire very soon, and they will be released after the Day of the Lord destruction begins. If you would like to know more about the giants, I would recommend the book by Steve Quayle called "*Genesis 6 Giants, Master Builders of Prehistoric and Ancient Civilizations.*"

How are men going to react when all of these things are released upon the earth? It's almost too much to comprehend. There will be a giant planet coming near the earth and causing untold destruction. Earthquakes, volcanoes and tsunamis raging throughout the world from the gravitational influence of the destroying planet will take down the electrical grid and all the comforts we presently rely upon. UFOs and the alien deception will become commonplace. Immortal beings will appear bent on the subjugation of men. Giants will be unleashed once again upon the earth and wreak havoc. All of these things happen when the Holy Spirit withdraws His protection because men have demanded that they want nothing to do with God.

The reaction of men was described in the Gospel of Luke:

> And there shall be signs in the sun, and in the moon, and in the stars; and upon the earth distress of nations, with perplexity; the sea and the waves roaring; men's hearts failing them for fear, and for looking after those things which are

coming on the earth: for the powers of heaven
shall be shaken. (Luke 21:25-26)

Rising up from the chaos and destruction on the earth, is
a man that will become known as the Mahdi. He is the man
destined to seize the day, a man that emerges to give hope
when there is none, a man talked about in many Scriptures
in the Bible. The antichrist is making his way upon the world
scene and few people are prepared for what will happen
when he arrives.

CHAPTER TWENTY-ONE
THE RISE OF THE ANTICHRIST

How does the antichrist rise to power? Does he rise from the ashes of the defeat of Gog? To refresh our memories, Gog and his massive army were immolated during the intervention of the Lord when they attacked Israel. Gog's carefully orchestrated Caliphate is gone along with him and his minions. The Muslim world stands at a critical cross road. There is no one to lead them. They have suffered the worst defeat in their history with the vast Islamic army destroyed on the plains and mountains of Israel.

To the Shiite Muslims awaiting the arrival of their long promised Twelfth Imam, the conditions are perfect for his arrival. It was promised long ago that the Twelfth Imam, or Mahdi, would arrive on the world scene after the Islamic world had suffered one of their worst defeats. The annihilation of Gog's gigantic Muslim army would certainly qualify as that event. No longer will the oppressed branch of Islam, the Shiites, have to force the appearance of the Twelfth Imam into reality. It is going to happen at this time and

Iran—the major power center for the Shiite Muslims—is going to benefit and be at the center of the world's attention once again. Now all the conditions are perfect for the rise of the man destined to rule the world.

Does it seem inconceivable that a leader backed by a minority branch of Islam based in Iran should rise to world prominence? Let's take a look at the conditions in the world at this time that allows it to happen.

▶ The leader of the Caliphate, Gog, and all his forces lie dead in Israel.

▶ The world has been rocked by a massive earthquake so powerful that it has affected every major land mass on the face of the earth.

▶ Accompanying this major earthquake will be catastrophic tsunamis.

▶ The largest tsunami on record struck Lituya Bay, Alaska, on July 9th, 1958 and reached a height of 1720 ft. That is close to the height of One World Trade Center in New York City (1776 ft.). The tsunamis generated by the great earthquake will meet or exceed this tsunami because of the effects of the great earthquake combined with the gravitational forces of the intruding planet. They will make the tsunamis in the Indian Ocean in December of 2004 and the Japanese tsunami of March 11, 2011 look like mere ripples in the ocean by comparison. Every coastal city in the world is going to be lying in ruins because of the devastating tsunamis generated by the worldwide earthquake. The damage and loss of life is going to be incalculable. All nations are going to be paralyzed by the unprecedented damage.

► The worldwide electrical grid will go down. People will be without power because of the damage caused by the earthquake. Access to water, proper sanitation, and food will be difficult to obtain. Starvation will become a gruesome reality.

► The infrastructure will be heavily damaged and the transportation of food and resources will become very difficult. Bridges and roads may be impassable for an extended period of time. Getting these things fixed will require a gargantuan effort made more difficult by the conditions in the world at that time.

► Death and disease will propagate out of control because of the lack of clean water and food. Fighting over basic resources will become the rule rather than the exception. Life will become tragic and difficult.

► The Holy Spirit will have been withdrawn from the earth and along with Him, the protection of the earth, the restraint of evil entities and forces, and those that had the Holy Spirit within them that had constantly cared for and helped other people—they too will be gone from the earth. With the bands of restraint lifted, evil forces and entities will flood the world wreaking havoc wherever they go. The times will be so troubling that men's hearts will fail them by the things coming into the world.

This is the background in which the antichrist will arise. Even the way the antichrist appears on the world scene is going to coincide with deceit and demonic forces. He is going to rise up out of a deep well in the earth as the conclusion of a process known as "occultation." What is occultation?

Occultation is a process that hides something, and then brings back whatever was hidden alive after an extended period—most likely through the usage of occult or dark forces. This is the exact term Shiite Muslims use to describe this process. This may seem like a bizarre and unlikely concept, but someone is going to arise from a deep well in the ground and claim to be the long-awaited Twelfth Imam or Mahdi.

By virtue of what has been written and said about this character, we immediately know two things about him. We know where he will appear, and we know what his real name will be. Let's examine where he will arise and what he will be called.

According to what has been written about the hidden Imam by Shiite Muslims, he will make his appearance from a well inside the Jamkaran Mosque in Iran. Muslims have been watching for his appearance from this deep well for hundreds of years. A constant vigil has been set up waiting for his arrival. Many expect a miraculous arrival through a process that stuns anyone witnessing the event. However it occurs, the Mahdi will arise from the depths of the well inside the Jamkaran Mosque in Iran. Here is what the Jamkaran Mosque looks like:

The Jamkaran Mosque in Iran from which the antichrist will appear after emerging from a well.

All of the Shiite prophecies predict that this is where he will arise from inside a deep well and then make his appearance known to the world.

The hidden Imam that emerges from the well has a history that is well known to Shiite Muslims. His father was the Eleventh Imam, Hasan al-Askari. He was an Imam that was held captive by the Abbasid Caliphate Al-Mu'tamid and was imprisoned in Samarra, Iraq from 846-874.[48] The office of the Caliphate at that time kept tight control over the Eleventh Imam, so much so that the Eleventh Imam sent his son into hiding in order to protect him. He didn't want his son to be controlled by the interference of the Caliphate, so his son was secreted away and disappeared from Samarra, Iraq where the Eleventh Imam was being held captive by the Caliphate.

---

48   Wikipedia, "Imamah (Shia Doctrine)," http://en.wikipedia.org/wiki/Imamah_(Shia_doctrine).

The one who was secreted away and disappeared is known as the Twelfth Imam. He was born on July 29th, 868 and went into occultation (hiding) in 872.[49] Devout Shiite Muslims like those in Iran have been awaiting his promised return ever since that time. The common belief among "Twelvers," those who believe in the return of the Twelfth Imam, is that the Twelfth Imam is going to come out of occultation (hiding) at a time of severe distress among the Islamic people. It is a time of chaos and pandemonium reigning on the face of the earth, and the Twelfth Imam is going to emerge to bring peace to the world and order out of chaos.

The long awaited Twelfth Imam has a name; it is **Muhammad ibn al-Hasan al-Mahdi**, but most will know him as **Muhammad al-Mahdi** or the **"Mahdi."** He has many titles that he is known by in the Islamic world such as "The Guided One," the "Hidden Imam," "The Proof," the "Lord of our Times," the "One vested with Divine Authority," "God's Remainder," and "The one who will rise and fill the universe with Justice."[50] To most of his followers, he will simply be called Mahdi. To almost everyone else in the world, he will eventually be known as the antichrist.

How is it possible that the one that will be known as the antichrist will be Islamic when most Christians today believe that the antichrist will be a European? Where did this misconception come from?

In the *Left Behind* series of books by Tim LaHaye and Jerry Jenkins, the antichrist is characterized as being European because of a prophecy given in the Old Testament Book of Daniel. In the ninth chapter, the antichrist is described as a prince who shall come and destroy the city and the

49   Ibid.
50   Ibid.

sanctuary. "And the people of the prince that shall come shall destroy the city and the sanctuary." (Daniel 9:26)

Who are the "people" of the prince that shall come [antichrist]? What city and sanctuary did they destroy?

In order to uncover the meaning behind this Scripture, we need to review a little history. We need to go to Israel after the time of Jesus's death on the cross when they rebelled against Rome. In the year 70 AD, the Roman General Titus led four legions of the Roman army and surrounded the city of Jerusalem. Titus was sent to quell the rebellion. He had his troops surround and lay siege to Jerusalem, and then waited until starvation and deprivation had taken their toll and weakened the citizens of Jerusalem.

After waiting a sufficient period of time, Titus had his four Roman legions attack. The defenders of Jerusalem were overwhelmed and the city was destroyed so completely that it was merely a shadow of the city it had once been. The temple of the Jewish people, their sanctuary, was burned to the ground and the rock walls that had once been a part of the temple were thrown down, in order to recover the melted gold that was in the crevices. Jerusalem [the city] and the temple [the sanctuary] were both destroyed in this attack.

Who were the people that destroyed Jerusalem and the temple? The "people" who destroyed Jerusalem and the temple were the people that comprised the four Roman legions. This is an important point. God wants us to recognize who these people were because they are the people of the future antichrist. They are the "people of the prince that shall come." Who were the people that comprised the four Roman legions that did all of the destruction?

Many Christian scholars have concluded that because they were Roman legions, the people that destroyed the temple were Europeans. Rome is based in Italy, so the logical conclusion is that Europeans destroyed Jerusalem and the temple. While this conclusion makes perfect sense, is it the correct conclusion to make without carefully examining the composition of the four Roman legions?

Let's dig a little deeper. We need to examine the ethnic background of the people that comprised the four Roman legions so we can understand where they came from. We need to remember an absolutely crucial point—there was an Eastern portion of the Roman Empire that we often overlook. The Eastern portion of the Roman Empire had legions that were comprised of people from the Middle East.

The people that comprised the four Roman Legions were predominately from the Middle East from an area that would eventually become Islamic. Here are the four legions and the composition of the troops making up each legion:

- The Tenth (X) legion called **Fretensis**— composed of people from Turkey and Syria, with Nabatean Arabs from West Jordan.

- The Fifteen (XV) legion called **Apollinaris**— gathered from the cohorts residing in Syria.

- The Twelfth (XII) legion called **Fulminata**— comprised of the people from the Melitene region of Eastern Turkey and Syria.

▶ The Fifth (V) legion called **Macedonia**—from the Moesia region south of the Danube River, composed of people from Serbia and Bulgaria.[51]

Almost all of these troops came from areas that are predominately Islamic in our day and age. They are Muslims and espouse different views of Islam, some Shiite and some Sunni, but they are all primarily Islamic countries.

With these new facts in mind, we can form some conclusions based on the analysis we have done. The antichrist (the prince who shall come) is not of European descent, but comes from the Eastern portion of the Roman Empire, and his people (the people of the prince that shall come) are Islamic and come from Islamic countries.

This may be a major paradigm shift for most people looking for the advent of the antichrist. They have been conditioned to believe that the antichrist is going to be European, but nothing could be further from the truth. Our analysis shows that the antichrist is going to be a leader of Islamic people, and will get his power base from Muslim nations. This also means that people looking for a revised Roman Empire to prepare the way for the antichrist are mistaken too. They should be looking for a revised Islamic Empire that prepares the way for the antichrist.

THE REVISED ISLAMIC EMPIRE

What we are seeing in the Islamic countries today—where Islam is rising up in conflict with the world—is exactly what the Bible predicted would happen in the last days.

---

51   Walid Shoebat and Joel Richardson, *God's War on Terror*, (New York, NY: Top Executive Media, 2008), p. 352.

212 | THE RISE AND FALL OF ISIS

This prediction was made in the last book of the Bible—Revelation. Let's take a look at what was said so we can gain some insight.

> They are also seven kings. Five have fallen, one is, the other has not yet come; but when he does come, he must remain for a little while. The beast who once was, and now is not, is an eighth king. He belongs to the seven and is going to his destruction. (Revelation 17:10-11)

Let's analyze what has been said here. This passage lets us know there are going to be a total of eight beast empires that will have ruled on earth before Jesus Christ returns again. The antichrist is the ruler of the eighth beast empire, and he is the one that once was, and is not, and yet somehow is once again. The antichrist was alive before, disappeared in 872, and is going to come back to life after being gone for almost 1200 years. What Revelation is describing is the process of occultation that we have discussed earlier. It is the exact process that brings this ruler back once again after a period of time where he has been in hiding. The process that brings the antichrist back is never explained, but it most likely happens through some sort of occult ritual. Astoundingly this Scripture says that the ruler of the eighth beast empire belongs to the seventh beast empire and comes out of the seventh empire. We can conclude from this statement that the antichrist was alive during the reign of the seventh beast empire, and comes out of a time when the seventh beast empire was in control of the world. In order for us to properly identify the antichrist, we need to know more about the beast empires—especially the seventh beast empire. Who were these beast empires?

We need more information so let's identify the beast empires so we can make sense out of this passage. At the time this passage was written by the Apostle John, five beast empires had already existed. They were:

1. The Egyptian Empire.

2. The Assyrian Empire.

3. The Babylonian Empire.

4. The Persian Empire.

5. The Greek Empire.

John tells us that one empire "is," and this is the sixth empire. What empire was in control of the world when the Apostle John wrote these things? The Roman Empire controlled most of the known world when John wrote these things.

The identification of the seventh beast empire is not as simple as the others, and yet its identification is critical to understand this Scripture. From what we are told in this verse, the seventh beast empire had not yet come in John's day. The Roman Empire was in control of the world in John's day and was the sixth empire. Every other empire preceding the Romans were conquered by the empire coming after them. For example the Egyptians were conquered by the Assyrians, the Assyrians were conquered by the Babylonians...and so on in that manner. If we really want to know who the seventh beast empire was, we need to ask: Who conquered the sixth empire, the Roman Empire?

What many people forget is the fact that the Roman Empire split in two in 395 AD, into a western and eastern portion.[52] The western portion of the Roman Empire fell far earlier than the eastern portion. The eastern portion of the Roman Empire continued almost a thousand years after the fall of the western half. The final vestiges of the Roman Empire fell in 1453 when the Muslim Turks under Mehemet II overran the city of Constantinople. Mehemet II represented the Turkish Caliphate of the Islamic empire. His success led to the formation of the Ottoman Empire, a distinctly Muslim Empire under the direction of the Caliphate.

So who conquered the Roman Empire? It was an Islamic Empire under the direction of the Caliphate that accomplished this feat. Based on this information, the seventh beast empire was an Islamic Empire under the direct control of the Caliphate. Therefore the antichrist will revive an Islamic Empire to become the eighth beast empire and it will have the characteristics of the seventh empire. The Apostle John told us this when he said the eighth beast empire would be "of the seventh." In other words, John is saying that the eighth beast empire would be composed of elements of the seventh beast empire, and would come out of the seventh beast empire.

Now it is easier to understand the background of the antichrist (Twelfth Imam). He fits the description given of the antichrist perfectly. He was alive before, went into hiding in 872 when the seventh beast empire under the Islamic Caliphate was in control, he is literally from the seventh beast empire, and is due to reappear on the world scene in the near future. No other person in history could possibly fit this description so precisely and accurately.

Now we can complete our list of the eight beast empires:

---

52   Walid Shoebat and Joel Richardson, *God's War on Terror*, (New York, NY: Top Executive Media, 2008), p. 302.

6. The Roman Empire.

7. The Islamic Empire under the direction of the Caliphate which became the Ottoman Empire.

8. An Islamic Empire under the direction of the Twelfth Imam and manifested in the antichrist.

THE FIRST ACTION OF THE TWELFTH IMAM

What will the Twelfth Imam (antichrist) do when he comes back and makes his appearance to the world? The first thing he will do is to assume control of the Islamic Caliphate. This book tracks the progress and fate of the power structure behind the rise of the Islamic Empire—the office of the Caliphate. The office of the Caliphate is not destroyed or phased out with the destruction of ISIS and the annihilation of Gog in Israel. Its power is too alluring to be abandoned after two defeats. Even after the office of the Caliphate is in shambles because Gog and his massive army will be destroyed on the plains and mountains of Israel, its power cannot be left alone. The antichrist is going to seize control of the office of the Caliphate. There is a leadership vacuum in the Caliphate at the time the Twelfth Imam takes control. He is going to do something that has rarely been done in the history of the Muslim religion. He is going to unite the office of the Twelfth Imam and the office of the Caliphate into one united voice leading the Islamic world.

The Muslim world has always had two horns of leadership vying for control of all of Islam. They are the office of the Caliphate and the office of the Imams. The antichrist will unite these two offices into one, uniting all the leadership of the Muslim world. The Bible predicted this would happen when it said the beast will have "two horns like a lamb."

(Revelation 13:11) In biblical terms, horns are a symbol of leadership. The Muslim world has always had two horns of leadership vying for control of all of Islam—the office of the Imams and the office of the Caliphate. Not only will the antichrist combine these two offices into one, but he will have all of the authority (the office of the Caliphate) and power of the first beast (Gog and his Islamic Empire.)

The Twelfth Imam or antichrist continues the office of the Caliphate and combines it with the office of the Imams so that all of Islam has a united voice leading them. This is the new power structure leading the Muslim world with the antichrist directing the way. What he is able to accomplish during his period of rule has been written about many times. Let's take a look at what can be expected when the antichrist controls the power structure guiding Islam.

CHAPTER TWENTY-TWO
THE REIGN OF THE ANTICHRIST

The Bible has much to say about the antichrist and what he does during his reign on the earth. People will assume he has the best intentions when he begins his rule. He will promise to fill the void in the lives of so many people on the earth—but this will be a promise he is unable to keep. There will be so much despair and destruction at the time of his arrival that people will be looking for someone to rescue and save them from their intolerable plight. The world will be reeling from the destructive events that have just occurred, many of the most helpful people in their communities with the guidance and direction of the Holy Spirit within them will be gone (taken in the rapture), and many people will have been killed during the destructive events of the great earthquake.

The antichrist will appear on the world scene promising peace and order in a time when there is none. He will have a receptive audience waiting for him. Anyone that can provide a ray of hope in the world's intolerable situation will be welcomed with open arms.

He will begin in a world full of desperation—where deceit and demonic forces rule because of the withdrawal of the Holy Spirit. He will promise order to a world out of control. He will promise to fill the void in the lives of so many people on the earth. This will be a promise he is unable to keep. His true nature will rise to the forefront, and soon he will not be able to stop himself from demonstrating his contempt for any that will not bend to the force of his will. He will not tolerate any that oppose him, and will actively move to suppress their opinions and their voice. He will quickly set himself up to be the ruler of the world and will stop at nothing to usurp the throne that is reserved for Jesus Christ.

We have not been left uninformed about how the antichrist arises and the way he achieves his pathway to power. God's Word is full of references about him. We need to review some of those references so we can understand more about him.

REFERENCES IN THE BIBLE ABOUT THE ANTICHRIST

1. **There is no doubt that he will be the continuation of the Islamic Beast Empire set up by Abu Bakr al-Baghdadi and Gog.** The Bible tells us the antichrist comes up "out of the earth" (Revelation 13:11) and "out of the bottomless pit." (Revelation 17:8) This aligns with Islamic hadiths that say their great leader will come up out of a bottomless well inside the Jamkaran Mosque in Iran. He too is pictured coming up out of the earth. This is not a coincidence. The

references to someone arising out of the earth in Revelation and the Islamic prophecies of the one coming out of the earth from a well in Iran are the same person—the antichrist.

2. **He rises to power through the occult, and uses the power of the occult to achieve his desires.** (Daniel 8:23-25) We need to elaborate on this point somewhat. The antichrist was hidden through a process known as "occultation." This is some form of secret and esoteric ritual involving the black arts which hides a person until the time of their revealing. Another ritual-istic satanic arts ceremony is required to bring the person out of hiding for their unveiling to the world. The antichrist will emerge following just such a ritual. The conclusion we can draw from this information is that the antichrist was hidden and will arise from some sort of satan-ic ritualistic process. This is precisely what a Scripture in Daniel is telling us. "A king of fierce countenance, and understanding dark sen-tences, shall stand up." (Daniel 8:23) In other words, the antichrist will have understanding of black magic and will come to power through the occult.

3. **The antichrist will have demonic power sup-porting him.** "And his power shall be mighty, but not by his own power." (Daniel 8:24) He will tap into the power of satanic sources and will be so comfortable with the satanic power at his disposal that he will encourage people to get involved with black magic, and to indulge in the satanic arts. "And through his policy also

he shall cause craft to prosper in his hand."
(Daniel 8:25) One thing is certain during the
reign of the antichrist—black magic and satanic rituals will become routine and commonplace
while he is in power.

4. **He overthrows three kings in order to come to
   power.** (Daniel 7:8) He will need to overthrow
   three rulers in positions of power to solidify his
   world dominion. We don't know who these rulers will be, but most likely they will be leaders
   in the Islamic world who want to control the
   office of the Caliphate. They will be defeated
   by the antichrist as he moves to control the
   entire world.

5. **The antichrist heals the deadly wound of the
   beast empire.** (Revelation 13:3) He does this
   by restoring the office of the Caliphate and
   the Imam. Gog had restored the office of the
   Caliphate and the antichrist restores the office of the Imam after it had been gone from
   the earth for such a long time. Without the
   leadership of either of these two offices, it
   was considered a terrible head wound to the
   Muslim world. The antichrist heals the wound
   and takes over as the leader of both of these
   offices.

6. **He comes promising peace to the world.** To
   accomplish this, the antichrist signs a peace
   treaty with the nation of Israel that he says
   will guarantee them peace in their time. (Daniel
   9:27) This act initiates the 70th week of Daniel,
   the final seven year period of time before Jesus
   returns to set up His kingdom in the world.

7. **The antichrist will deceive and destroy many by the peace treaty he sets up.** (Daniel 8:25) The world will be craving peace and order after the rampage of Gog and the devastation of the great earthquake. This peace treaty will allow him to do as he wishes, and by his peaceful deceit he will be able to destroy whomever he chooses, in order to perpetuate the illusion of peace.

8. **The antichrist will set up world dominion.** He wants to rule the world, and he will be able to achieve this goal. The Bible says "Power was given him over all kindreds, and tongues, and nations." (Revelation 13:7)

9. **To demonstrate his power and control over the world, the antichrist will cause all to receive a mark of his beast empire.** (Revelation 13:16) This point needs further clarification. One thing we need to remember is the fact that the antichrist is the Twelfth Imam. All eleven Imams before him had marks or symbols that signified their power and these marks were worn by their followers. It is perfectly normal for the Twelfth Imam to demand that all of his followers be identified by his mark or symbol also. The Bible says that this mark will be placed in their right hand or forehead and will distinguish all those that have this mark as a follower of the antichrist. The antichrist will use this identification mark as some sort of control for regulating everything that you need in life to survive. People will not be able to buy anything such as food and basic goods without

using this mark. In this way the antichrist will have power over all people, and will probably receive some revenue stream whenever this mark is employed. Somehow the symbol he uses is associated with the number 666. The Bible describes this in the following way: "He also forced everyone, small and great, rich and poor, free and slave, to receive a mark on his right hand or on his forehead, so that no one could buy or sell unless he had the mark, which is the name of the beast or the number of his name. This calls for wisdom. If anyone has insight, let him calculate the number of the beast, for it is man's number. His number is 666." (Revelation 13:16-18 NIV)

The Apostle John warned us that no person should ever receive the mark that the anti-christ demands you take. If you do, you will be subject to the wrath of God that will be poured out in the bowl and trumpet judgments and you will be separated from God forever. (Revelation 14:9-11)

10. **He will wage war against the saints, and will overcome them.** (Revelation 13:7) Where do these saints come from and why is he able to overcome them? Not all of the people in the churches are going to be protected by the rapture. There are too many people in the churches today who do not have the Holy Spirit within them and lack the guidance that the Holy Spirit can provide. They do whatever they feel is right in their own eyes. They have no idea what the Bible actually says or that

there is a chapter in the Bible that tells you what to do and what not to do to receive the guidance of the Holy Spirit. (Galatians 5:16-26) Those who do not have the Holy Spirit within them live by an irrational set of rules that neither justifies nor protects them when the destructive events associated with the Day of the Lord comes upon them. Consequently they have missed the rapture and are described as being lukewarm, unwise, and those that will be thrown into the great tribulation. As we reviewed the letters to the seven churches, many church goers are characterized in this manner, and numerous warnings were given them to change their ways or face the consequences of the great tribulation. No doubt these people who have some knowledge of the Bible will realize their error after the rapture has occurred. They will finally turn to the Lord but will face a horrific time and will face the onslaught of the antichrist. The saints being referenced in this Scripture are the ones that fall into this category, and while they are trying to change their ways and follow Jesus as best they can in their new circumstances; they will find it extremely difficult and many will be overcome by the antichrist's wanton destruction of Christians and Jews.

11. **The antichrist will change times and laws.** (Daniel 7:25) This is a reference that makes no sense until we realize what has happened just prior to the antichrist arriving on the world scene. When the destruction associated with the Day of the Lord begins, a great earthquake

is going to shake the entire world. This earthquake is going to be so severe that "the earth shall remove out of her place." (Isaiah 13:13) This means that the orbit of the earth is going to be disrupted. There are numerous sources that have stated that the earth moving out of its stationary orbit in the past has been caused by the earth interacting with a planet-sized body in a cosmic close encounter. This is why the Vatican is so diligently watching a large planet-sized body approaching the earth with their infrared telescope called Lucifer on Mt. Graham. When this huge planet gets close enough, we will have the exact effects described in Ezekiel 38 and 39 and Revelation chapter 6. There will be a global earthquake and sheets of fire falling out of the skies as volatile compounds from space fall into our atmosphere and are ignited by fiery meteorites. The sun will be darkened and the moon will turn blood red.

Another deadly effect of the rogue planet passing close by the earth will be the impact of the gravitational forces exerted by the intruding planet. The gravitational forces will be so intense that the orbit of the earth will be affected and shortened. This is going to have a tremendous impact on the earth because the gravitational pull of the passing body could shorten our orbit until it resembles the orbit the earth used to have in ancient days. In the book *Catastrophism and the Old Testament*, Donald Patten cites that every ancient culture had years that were 360 days in length. This includes Arabia, Assyria, Babylonia, China, Egypt, Greece, India, Japan, Mexico, Palestine, Persia, Peru, and early Rome.[53] Every one of these cultures had years that were 360 days in length. This is the basis for 360 degrees in a circle. As a consequence of the earthquake and cosmic encounter, which will shorten the orbit of the earth, the antichrist will need to change time to accurately reflect the true period of the year which will change to 360 days a year.

Another place that verifies the earth's new orbit will be 360 days a year is found in the book of Daniel. Daniel tells us that the time in which the antichrist enters the Jewish temple, stops the daily sacrifice and desecrates the Jewish temple is going to be the midpoint of the final seven year period of time, or three-and-a-half years into the seven-year period. Revelation then specifies the number of days that will be—and it says that it is exactly 1260 days. (Revelation 12:6) The only way three and a half years totals 1260 days is by having a calendar year of 360 days, not the current 365 ¼ days we have now. (See Revelation 12:6 and Daniel 9:27) Therefore, sometime before the appearance of the antichrist, earth's orbit is going to be shortened to 360 days a year.
The way the antichrist changes laws is by instituting Sharia Law in the areas he controls. Sharia Law is the moral code and religious law of the Islamic Religion. It is characterized by

---

53   Donald Wesley Patten, *Catastrophism and the Old Testament*, (Seattle, WA: Pacific Meridian Publishing Company, 1988), pp. 221-222.

harsh punishments such as flogging, stoning, and the cutting off of one's hands for more serious infractions. This is strictly an Islamic law, and reinforces the fact that the antichrist is going to be the Islamic religion.

12. **The antichrist shall not regard the God of his fathers, nor the desire of women.** (Daniel 11:37) This is another point that needs further clarification. Many have said that the fact the antichrist does not regard the desire of women means that he is homosexual. When we closely examine this Scripture, a more accurate interpretation may mean that women have such insignificant standing in the hierarchy of the antichrist's religion that he doesn't care what they want or desire. The Islamic culture is centered around men, with the desires of women being a secondary concern. In this way, the antichrist does not regard the desire of women. The fact that the antichrist does not regard the "God of his fathers" should be disturbing to those in the Muslim religion. This probably means that the antichrist is not driven by the teachings of Islam as much as he is driven to use all means at his disposal to accomplish his goals. The Bible says he will "Honor the god of forces" (Daniel 11:38) and that he shall acknowledge a "strange god." (Daniel 11:39) What is meant by a "strange god"? If we combine what these two Scriptures are saying then we can conclude that some sort of strange god is going to appear that somehow has control of the forces around him. Is this referring to some sort of "alien deception" or UFO

disclosure? Is the antichrist going to rise to power on the heels of some sort of alien disclosure that will shock the world into believing in some foreign alien god?

We already know the antichrist arises to take power through some sort of ritual of the occult. This ritual will be satanic in nature and we know that satanic forces use deception as a common means to accomplish their purposes. The minions of Satan could be posing as an alien presence to orchestrate a grand delusion that casts doubt on the religious history of the world. The antichrist, being the opportunist that he is, will use the deceptive masquerade of the alien presence to cement and consolidate his rise to power, and in this way will fulfill the Scripture where it says he will not regard the God of his fathers (Daniel 11:37) but will acknowledge a strange god that is a god of forces. The most recent book that has proposed this theory is *Exo-Vaticana* by Chris Putnam and Thomas Horn. The other book proposing the same theory is *Alien Encounters* by Chuck Missler and Mark Eastman. Both books provide excellent documentation to support this theory of alien deception by demonic forces and I would encourage you to read them if you would like more information on this subject.

13. **The antichrist will be a great deceiver.** (2 Thessalonians 2:11) He comes into the world in a time when the Holy Spirit has been withdrawn and the restraint against evil forces has been removed. Deceit will rule the day and the

truth will be hard to find. The antichrist will arrive promising peace, but he will promote the most war-like conditions ever found on the face of the earth. Everyone that does not agree with him is marked for extermination.

14. **He will show signs and lying wonders.** (2 Thessalonians 2:9) This can be accomplished by the assistance of occult forces— or by the assistance of a deceptive alien presence which is really satanic powers manifesting a great delusion.

15. **He will cause fire to come down from heaven.** (Revelation 13:13) This point must be commented upon. One of the things that the Lord will do to protect the nation of Israel when the armies of Gog are arrayed against them is to cause fire to fall from heaven to destroy the coalition of Magog. The rain of fire from heaven is a method that the Lord used to protect His people. The antichrist will be claiming that he is God, so it is natural he will try to mimic the power of God by doing something that God has done. He will be able to cause fire to come down from heaven by the power of the satanic forces at his disposal. Satan is always trying to mimic things the Lord has done and because the antichrist is an agent of Satan, he will have the ability to make fire come down from heaven also.

16. **The antichrist will have the ability to give life to inanimate objects.** (Revelation 13:15) What in the world does this mean? How is it possible to give life to inanimate objects? Before

we comment on this, let's review what the Scripture has to say. "And he had power to give life unto the image of the beast, that the image of the beast should both speak, and cause that as many as would not worship the image of the beast should be killed." (Revelation 13:15) This is a clear reference to the application of artificial intelligence, and can be the result of design or demonic possession. People are going to be making images (idols), and then these images are going to have artificial intelligence capabilities place within them that are demonic in nature. This is clear because when the images speak, they are going to say that people should be killed if they are not worshipping the demonically imbued idols that represent the antichrist. This will be a way the antichrist will be able to exert control over the world and will enable him to discover all those that are not worshipping him.

17. **He will set himself up to be worshipped as God in the Jewish temple.** (2 Thessalonians 2:4) This is one of the milestone events that occur in the life of the antichrist. Three and a half years into the seven year period that fulfills Israel's destiny (Daniel 9:27), the antichrist is going to enter the Jewish temple. This means that the Jewish temple will be rebuilt sometime before the antichrist arrives of the world scene. He will proceed into the Holy of Holies, a place reserved for God, and will set himself up to be worshiped as God. This act is going to be known as the abomination of desolation, or the abomination that makes desolate. No one

is ever to be in the Holy of Holies in the Jewish temple except the High Priest on one day in the year. This is a place reserved for God. The fact that the antichrist enters it is a desecration of the Jewish temple. God looks on this as an abomination. The antichrist wants to be worshipped by the entire world as God, and entering and setting himself up to be worshipped in the Jewish temple is a natural way for him to make that proclamation.

This act allows many in the house of Israel who have been misled to see the antichrist for who he really is—a great deceiver. When those in Israel realize his true identity, some will escape from the city of Jerusalem as the antichrist's forces move to seal off the city. They will flee to a place where God will protect them (Isaiah 26:20) while the Lord unleashes a great destruction upon the whole earth. (Isaiah 28:22) The Lord's anger (Isaiah 26:20) is consistent with the trumpet and vial judgments we see described in Revelation.

18. **The antichrist will lead the world's armed forces in the Battle of Armageddon.** (Revelation 16:16) As his final act of defiance, the antichrist will gather the world's armed forces and lead an attack against Israel. When the Lord responds, the antichrist will not know what hit him. As he and the armies of the world prepare to attack Israel, they will be overwhelmed by Jesus Christ leading the armies of the Lord. Armageddon will not be much of a war because the armies of the antichrist will be

destroyed almost immediately by the forces that the Lord brings against them. Revelation tells us:

Then I saw the beast and the kings of the earth and their armies gathered together to make war against the rider on the horse and his army. But the beast was captured, and with him the false prophet who had performed the miraculous signs on his behalf. With these signs he had deluded those who had received the mark of the beast and worshiped his image. The two of them were thrown alive into the fiery lake of burning sulfur. The rest of them were killed with the sword that came out of the mouth of the rider on the horse. (Revelation 19:19-21 NIV)

In this way the reign of the antichrist will come to an end. His rule will be limited to seven years, and his forces will be defeated in the Battle of Armageddon. He will be defeated by Jesus Christ who will return to the earth at His Second Coming. The antichrist's brief career as ruler of the world will be brought to an end when the rightful heir of the world comes to take the throne that He paid for with His own blood.

THE FINAL END OF THE OFFICE OF THE CALIPHATE

This is the end of all of those who would rule the world through the office of the Caliphate. From Abu Bakr al-Baghdadi, to Gog, and then finally to the antichrist, each will seize control of the Caliphate only to have the power the office holds wrenched from their grasp. Each will be defeated after some initial success. The power of the office of the Caliphate will be vanquished when Jesus Christ returns to the world once more and assumes the throne of David in Israel.

There is a fundamental law that should be observed by the adherents of any religion. **You do not have the right in the name of any religion to go out and kill others, or force others to convert to your religion unwillingly.** If your religion can only gain converts by the force of the sword, then by force of the sword that religion will be destroyed. The leader of ISIS, Gog, and the antichrist should remember this in their quest to rule the world.

In the end, the house of Israel emerges victorious and takes their rightful position in the world. Those raptured return to the earth when the Lord returns and are forever with the Lord. Finally there will be peace on earth and goodwill to all men. The promise of Jesus Christ will be fulfilled.

CHAPTER TWENTY-THREE
THE REVERSE 9/11

In September of 2015, there were three signs that converged in one month, signaling a change was coming upon the world. They were the culmination of the four blood moons, the end of the Shemitah year and a solar eclipse. In my book, *Fifteen Days in September That Will Change the World*, I stated that these signs were a time of caution for the world, and proposed a series of events that could be a time of trouble for the United States and the Middle East starting on 9/11 in 2015.

I documented how in times past, the manifestation of these signs had a detrimental effect on the United States. For example, the end of the two previous Shemitah years coincided with the collapse of the stock market which had an extreme negative impact on our economy. The attacks on 9/11 in the year 2001, which brought down the Twin Trade Towers, came near the conclusion of a Shemitah cycle. The four blood moon tetrads of the past had signaled a time of change for the nation of Israel because they appeared on

Jewish Holy days when Israel formed their nation (1948) and when Israel fought and gained more land in the Six Day War (1967).

And yet the signs came in September of 2015 with no noticeable impact on the United States or its economy. Were these signs truly a warning of something that would take place—or were they merely a curiosity signifying nothing of consequence?

Sometimes we are so focused on an event that we concentrate on the wrong place, and fail to see what is happening in other places in the world. This was one of those times because September in 2015 was absolutely devastating to another country in the world. It was the country from which the majority of the 9/11 hijackers came from and the country that shares responsibility for the attacks on 9/11 in the United States. It is the country of Saudi Arabia.

FIFTEEN DAYS IN SEPTEMBER IN SAUDI ARABIA

What happened in Saudi Arabia in September of 2015 can most accurately be described as the reverse 9/11. It began on a date of infamy to the United States. On September 11th, 2015, something unusual happened in Mecca at the site of the Grand Mosque that was caught on camera. Pictures and video recorded the following image:

Lightning strikes a Crane in Mecca on 9/11 in Saudi Arabia

A lightning bolt struck a crane operating near the Grand Mosque in Mecca, Saudi Arabia. This was just a prelude to something that would happen later in the day. At around 5 PM, a fierce wind storm began to form. The skies darkened and sand was blown around by the gusting winds. The storm increased in intensity and people began to take cover, shocked by the severity of the storm. The winds increased in force until the sounds of tearing and grinding metal could be heard amidst the howling gusts. A huge crane wrenched free of its restraints and crashed through a portion of the Grand Mosque, killing 107 people immediately.

Crane crashes through a portion of the Grand Mosque in Mecca,
Saudi Arabia on 9/11, 2015.

What was most unusual was that there were about 100 cranes operating in Mecca at this time. This particular crane was owned by the Bin Laden group; by the father of Osama Bin Laden and was part of the construction conglomerate owned in whole by the Bin Laden family.[54] Osama Bin Laden was the man most responsible for coordinating the attacks that devastated the United States on 9/11. Most of the people he recruited came from Saudi Arabia. It is absolutely astonishing that a crane owned by the Bin Laden family would crash through the holiest Mosque in Islam and cause death and destruction in the country where most of the attackers on 9/11 came from and that it would happen on the exact same date of the original attack—9/11. Astounding!!! This crane crash was rated the deadliest crane crash to ever happen in the world.

THE CRUSH OF THE CROWDS

54   Gina Cassini, "Breaking: You Won't Believe Who Owned the Crane That Collapsed in Mecca on 9/11 Anniversary," Top Right News, 12 September 2015, http://toprightnews.com/breaking-you-wont-believe-who-owned-the-crane-that-collapsed-in-mecca-today/.

THE REVERSE 9/11 | 237

A total of 111 people died in this tragedy, and while this event alone was horrific, it was not the end of events that would rock the nation of Saudi Arabia in September. Thirteen days later on September 24th, 2015, the most tragic event ever to happen in the history of the hajj pilgrimage took place. The hajj pilgrimage is where devoted Muslims travel to Mecca to walk around the site of the Kaaba—the holiest shrine in all of Islam. On September 24th, large crowds of people began surging forward in their walk to the Kaaba until there was no longer any room for them to move. The crush of the crowds degenerated into a stampede until people began to be crushed from the weight of the surging masses. Before order was restored, 2411 people were crushed to death at Mina. This is the number of deaths according to Al Jazeera America and the associated press.[55]

Just like many had been crushed in the collapse of the Twin Trade Towers, many were crushed by the surging of the crowds in Mecca on 9/11 of 2015.

Saudi Arabia has refused to release the official number of people killed in this tragedy because of the enormity of the disaster. The Saudis have steadfastly insisted that only 769 people died during the stampede in order to down-play their responsibility in failure to properly manage the crowds.[56] The associated press and Al Jazeerah arrived at the true number of those who died by tabulating the fatalities reported by each country that had citizens attending the hajj. The loss of life in this disaster was enormous and many nations blamed Saudi Arabia for this debacle.

---

55   The Associated Press, "Over 2,400 killed in September Saudi hajj stampede," Al Jazeera America, 10 December 2015, http://america.aljazeera.com/articles/2015/12/10/over-2400-killed-in-saudi-hajj-stampede.html.
56   Ibid.

ECONOMIC DISASTER

One of the goals of the 9/11 hijackers that attacked the United States was to collapse the economy of the US along with the Twin Trade Towers. The attackers wanted to deliver an economic blow that would cripple the financial institutions of our country. They wanted to create a financial disaster from which we would never recover.

As the dust settled from both of the tragedies that happened in Saudi Arabia in September of 2015, something else happened that placed Saudi Arabia on the brink of financial disaster. It was something that experts the world over said could never happen again. **The price of oil collapsed**. It didn't just fall a little, it plunged to the point where most countries could not cover the price of oil production. The price of oil collapsed so dramatically that Saudi Arabia, the country known the world over as the king of oil producers, was left scrambling for a way to keep its economy from imploding. Saudi Arabia had to borrow money just to keep their economy functioning for the first time in their history.

The beginning of the collapse of oil prices occurred in the fall of 2015 and continued on through the winter of 2016, placing Saudi Arabia in a precarious economic position. The financial malady continues on at this time.

OBSERVATIONS ABOUT THE REVERSE 9/11

Even the most casual of observers can't help but notice similarities of what happened to Saudi Arabia starting on 9/11 in 2015 and the events perpetrated against the United States by citizens of Saudi Arabia on 9/11, 2001. The difference in these two events is the fact that angry

Americans did not perpetrate any acts of hostility against the nation of Saudi Arabia. The United States went out of its way not to retaliate against Saudi Arabia. Yet the similarities between these two events are almost impossible to ignore. Let's consider the following facts about the reverse 9/11 that happened in Saudi Arabia:

- ▶ A lightning bolt struck a crane in Mecca on 9/11 in 2015. Lightning strikes have been signified as an "act of God" by almost every culture in the world. The fact that the lightning struck a "crane" would become significant later on in the day.

- ▶ A severe weather phenomenon developed late in the afternoon on 9/11 that quickly became a ferocious wind storm. The wind storm toppled a crane that crashed into the Grand Mosque killing 107 people immediately. The Grand Mosque is the holiest shrine in all of Islam and contains the Kaaba within its walls. Four more people died later from the injuries sustained in the event. People witnessing the event called it an "act of God."

- ▶ The crane that collapsed was owned by the Bin Laden family. Osama Bin Laden's father owned the construction conglomerate that operated the crane that collapsed. As a result of this incident, the Bin Laden construction conglomerate was cited and held responsible for the accident. Their construction contracts were suspended until they could demonstrate compliance to all safety codes enforced by Saudi Arabia. Osama Bin Laden's father pleaded that he could not be held responsible for an "act of God" and pleaded for leniency at the hands of the Saudi court system. It is unknown what the outcome of these proceedings is at this time.

▶ On September 24th, 2015, a crowd in Mina on the outskirts of Mecca began their walk toward the Kaaba, the Holy Shrine of the Islamic religion. No one knows how it began exactly, but the mass of people began surging forward until there was a literal stampede of people pushing forward. At least 2411 people were killed in the crush caused by the crowds in a tally tabulated by the associated press. There are still scores of people that have not been accounted for and are still missing according to the countries from which these people maintained citizenship.[57] This was the deadliest disaster that has ever happened in history of the hajj pilgrimage.

▶ The amount of people who perished in the Saudi Arabian reverse 9/11 event is approaching the same number of people who died in the 9/11 events in the United States. The irony is that many of these people are still missing and unaccounted for—just like the bodies of those who perished in the collapse of the Twin Trade Towers. Their bodies were simply gone and unrecoverable.

▶ The fact that these events happened on the same day that the attacks were perpetrated

---

57   Ibid.

on the United States is astounding! Citizens of Saudi Arabia carried out an attack on the United States on 9/11 in 2001, and on 9/11 in 2015 events overwhelmed the country of Saudi Arabia.

- ► The price of oil collapsed on world markets in the fall of 2015 sending the economy of Saudi Arabia into a downward spiral. The financial disaster intended for the United States in 2001 is now affecting the economy of the Saudis in 2015. With a glut of oil still on world markets, it is uncertain when the economic malaise of the world's oil markets will end.

GOD HOLDS PEOPLE AND NATIONS ACCOUNTABLE

For any who think that God does not hold people and nations accountable for their actions, they need to rethink this based on what has happened to Saudi Arabia in September of 2015. What happened to them is best described as a reverse 9/11.

This is a message to all those who will kill others to reach their goals and aspirations. You will be held accountable for your actions. It may not happen right away, and it may take years for your actions to catch up to you, but you will be held accountable eventually.

This is why the actions of the office of the Caliphate of Abu Bakr al-Baghdadi are doomed to failure. He has killed more people than can be imagined and has done this in the most despicable ways. This is why Gog and his Magog coalition of armies will never see their dreams come to fruition. His office of the Caliphate will kill more people than all other despots ruling the world ever have. The antichrist will arrive on the world scene promising peace to all people, but will soon degenerate into one of the worst mass murderers the world has ever seen. He too will fail because he does not regard the lives of others as having any value.

This is the fate awaiting all those who will lead the office of the Caliphate. They will have their time, but it will soon fade. They will disappear like a flower quickly fading and like a vapor in the wind.

Jesus Christ is destined to rule the world, and sometime in the near future He will come back to take His proper place as the ruler the world has so desperately longed for. All will look to Jesus and He will govern the way all of us expect in our leaders. He will be the King of Kings and the Lord of Lords.

CHAPTER TWENTY-FOUR
COMMON MISPERCEPTIONS THAT CAN BE DETRIMENTAL

There are a few final words I would like to leave with you. There are some common misperceptions that can be detrimental to you and your loved ones if you do not recognize them. There are some things that can be misconstrued when they happen that will draw you away from the path the Lord has placed you on if you do not recognize them for what they are. We must stay the course and be patient when things are happening all around us. The more you understand about the times that lay before us, the more of a resource you can be to your friends and family. In times of chaos and challenge, those who know what to expect can be a guiding light to all those around them. They can be a voice of calm in a sea of uncertainty.

With this in mind, let's review some important concepts that may help all of us in the future. When you know what to expect, the times before us will not be as challenging as to those who do not know what the Bible has warned us about. Here are some of those important points:

- **Not all wars in the future are the Battle of Armageddon.** From a brief review of the wars documented in the Bible, we can expect the Psalm 83 War and the Battle of Gog and Magog to take place before the final end-times Battle of Armageddon. Look at where the war is taking place and the composition of the armies involved in the battle for further confirmation. The Psalm 83 war details a battle between Israel and its immediate neighbors we see surrounding Israel today. The Gog/Magog war describes a battle by a leader arising in Turkey and leading a powerful Turkish/Islamic alliance. The Battle of Armageddon is led by the antichrist after he arises in the Islamic world as a peacemaker. Thinking that the Psalm 83 war or the Gog/Magog war is Armageddon will have you looking for the wrong things at the wrong time.

- **Not all powerful leaders that arise are the antichrist.** It seems that the popular thing to do currently is to identify all leaders with nefarious characteristics as the antichrist. The Bible tells us there have been many that fit the characteristics of the antichrist, "Even now many antichrists have come." (1 John 2:18 NIV) Certainly the ancient Roman ruler Nero fit that description, as well as Napoleon and Adolf Hitler. All of these men had despicable qualities and contempt for human life that qualifies them as an "antichrist." The antichrist that is referred to in this book arises out of the earth through a process of the occult and "uses peace to destroy many." (Daniel 8:25) He will most likely be charming, intelligent and extremely attractive. His true colors will emerge as he tries to force his will on others, and he will become possessed by the devil in his final quest for power before he is stopped by the return of Jesus Christ.

► **The antichrist is not European.** The antichrist arises from the eastern leg of the Roman Empire and his people come from that area also. The people of the antichrist are from areas which in our day are distinctly Islamic and are the ancestors of the forces that comprised the four Roman Legions that conquered Jerusalem in 90 AD. The antichrist arises from among the Muslim nations and his forces are Islamic. He will be an Islamic antichrist.

► **The pope is not the false prophet.** Many have proposed that the pope is the false prophet of Revelation—but that simply is not the case. We are not here to debate the merits of what the pope has done or not done—or to dwell on any hidden agenda of the Catholic Church. The current pope may make bad decisions and may propose a questionable agenda—but that does not make him the false prophet. It makes him a man with a multitude of failures just like the rest of us. The actual false prophet is active today and is telling the rabbis in Israel that he is Jesus Christ and that he will make his appearance official sometime in the near future. He will point the way to the Islamic antichrist and will show many signs and lying wonders to authenticate this claim. Don't believe the things that he says. The actual false prophet will direct Islamic forces to Rome where the pope will be killed and the Catholic Church will be prevented from electing another pope to take his place. The false prophet will proclaim that the followers of the Catholic religion should follow the antichrist and that the antichrist is their new pope.

► **Mystery Babylon is not Rome.** Nor is it New York or any other city that has been misclassified with this designation. Mystery Babylon has to be a city within the Muslim Empire and has to be a city where the worship of a false religion is glorified and the object of that worship is adorned in purple and scarlet and decked with gold and precious stones and pearls. (Revelation 17:4) It is a city that sits on seven hills (Revelation 17:9) and a city whose destruction can be heard in the Red Sea. (Jeremiah 49:21) The only city that qualifies on all these counts is the city of Mecca in Saudi Arabia. The city of Mecca is home to the Kaaba—a black meteorite stone that has been worshipped and revered by Muslims since the inception of their religion. Just like Jesus Christ has been the rock of the Christian religion (Psalm 18:31) and the person Christians can place their faith in, Satan tries to mimic this by providing an actual rock that represents a false system of worship. The enclosure housing the Kaaba is covered in scarlet and purple on a dark background and adorned with gold, pearls and precious stones. The door to the black meteorite is made of 280 kilograms of pure gold. Blasphemous phrases are etched in silver threads and gold inlays across the covering of the Kaaba. The Kaaba is literally covered in phrases blaspheming God. Mystery Babylon lies in a city that was founded on seven hills. Mecca has seven hills and those hills are called the following: 1) Jabal abu Siba', 2) Jabal Safa, 3) Jabal Marwah, 4) Jabal abu Milhah, 5) Jabal abu Ma'aya, 6) Jabal abu Hulayah, and 7) Jabal abu Ghuzlan. These are the seven hills of Mecca and Mecca fulfills the prophecy saying that Mystery Babylon is a city comprised of seven hills. (Revelation 17:9) Furthermore, when the Lord judges Mystery Babylon and it is destroyed by the Lord, the destruction of it can be heard in the Red Sea. (Jeremiah 49:21) This is a geographical marker telling us where to look for Mystery Babylon. Mecca is located near the Red Sea as anyone can clearly see by looking at a map. It is the only city of biblical importance that is located near the Red Sea and the only city close enough to the Red Sea so that its destruction can be heard on this body of water. For all of these reasons Mystery Babylon can be identified as Mecca, the spiritual heart of a false religious system located in Saudi Arabia. The reverse 9/11 was a prelude to the destruction that awaits Mecca if Islamic radicals don't stop the slaughter of their fellowman. It is also the reason for the image on the cover of this book.

► **Because we are in the 70th Jubilee year does not mean we can know when the next war happens in Israel.** There have been many signs given recently (Four Blood Moons and the end of the Shemitah year) and it is true that we are currently in the 70th Jubilee year cycle, but that does not dictate when the Lord can accomplish His purposes or when He allows the next war to happen. The next war, the Psalm 83 war, could happen during the 70th Jubilee year cycle which ends in October of 2016, or it could happen well beyond that time. Only the Lord knows when the timing is right. There have been things of major importance to Israel that have happened in the two previous Jubilee year cycles, such as the liberation of Jerusalem from the Ottoman Turks by General Allenby in 1917, and the Six Day War in 1967 that gave the capital city of Jerusalem back to Israel. This does not mean that the perfect timing of the Lord must be limited to the duration of the 70th Jubilee year. The next war may happen sometime during this year, or it may not. When the Lord allows the next war to occur, it will be the perfect timing for this war and we will understand it after the war has happened.

► **There is no way to determine when the rapture takes place.** It is true that there will be a great earthquake in the future. The Lord will take the people with the Holy Spirit within them to be with Him before He allows that to take place. But if you think you can time this event or determine when it will happen you are sadly mistaken. No one knows the Lord's timing of this event or the hour or the day when it occurs. (Matthew 24:36) You can however know the overall conditions that will be prevalent in the world when this event happens. The important thing is to always be ready and to change your life now so you can have the gift of the guidance of the Holy Spirit now in your life. This gift is free to any believer and follower of Jesus Christ and to any church member that accepts Jesus Christ as their Savior and acknowledges their sin. Don't miss out having the Holy Spirit as a part of your life. He will change your life and the lives of everyone around you including your friends and family. Take advantage of the gift of the Holy Spirit while He is still available to you.

▶ **The Holy Spirit has been protecting us from far more than we know.** There are some truly disastrous events waiting to happen that have been held back by the power and influence of the Holy Spirit. When the Holy Spirit leaves and His protecting influence is withdrawn, mankind will truly experience what it means to not have God in their lives. It will literally become a Hell on earth. The age of deception, destruction and slaughter will overtake the earth. Man's wish to not have God interfering in his life will be granted and a series of destructive events will manifest across the globe. If these times were not shortened then no people would be left alive. (Matthew 24:22) An alien deception will masquerade across the globe, a destroying planet will have a cosmic close encounter with the earth, and giants will be released from their prison inside the earth and will rampage across the planet killing as many people as they can (Enoch 15:9-10). Plagues and famine will devastate the earth and the world will enter a time of unending warfare. Men's hearts will fail them from seeing the things that are coming upon the earth. (Luke 21:26) It will become a time that is terrible to be alive. You do not have to be a part of this time—it is your choice. Accept Jesus Christ as your Savior, admit and repent of your sins and then ask for the guidance and direction of the Holy Spirit in your life. If you do those things, you will be spared from the challenging times just described.

FINAL THOUGHTS

We live in a world that is largely unprepared for the challenges that lie ahead. We also live in a time that the Bible has tried to prepare us for. We have been given many answers to the perplexing times that await us, the problem is that few are trying to seek these answers from the greatest resource we have available to us—the Bible. As situations in the world begin to escalate out of control, men and women will begin to seek answers to life's most challenging questions. They will go to whoever can provide those answers.

This book has been an attempt to provide answers to these questions based on a biblical perspective. It has been an attempt to provide us with a different perspective and get us to see things from a Middle Eastern point of view. The research behind this book took many years to gather and came from multiple different resources. It was designed to inform you and make you a fountain of information to those that have questions in the days that await us. Some of the topics presented were frightening and unsettling. Others give us hope and encouragement when it's hard to see the victory that awaits us. All of the information in this book was designed to give insight and provide answers to troubling questions. The more you are informed, the more you can help others in their time of questions and need.

A CHALLENGE TO THE READER

If you have found this book worthwhile and informative, I have a special request for you. There is no vast publishing empire supporting me, or people employed to get this message out. I rely on people like you to tell others about the message of this book and to encourage others to read it. If you have the resources, buy multiple copies and give the book to your friends and family. It may be the thing that lets them know they can trust Jesus Christ and the Bible as the challenges of the end-time overwhelm all of us.

I have chosen to stay out of the spotlight on social media sites. People have told me that you cannot succeed with a book without a relentless marketing campaign. I firmly believe that the message contained on the pages of this book is far more important than the messenger. If what is written is impactful enough, then, with your help, there is no way anyone can stop it. Helping others gain understanding is the most worthwhile thing I can do and this book was written with the express purpose of drawing people to Jesus Christ and letting others know you can trust Jesus in the days ahead.

May the Lord guide us all on our journey through life, and may He bless and keep us all.

Made in the USA
San Bernardino, CA
23 May 2016